The
FOCALGUIDE
to
Shooting Animation

THE (f) FOCALGUIDES TO

The
FOCALGUIDE
to
Shooting Animation

Zoran Perisic

Focal Press

London & New York

© Focal Press Limited 1978

ISBN 0 240 50973 0

British Library Cataloguing in Publication Data

Perisic, Zoran
    The focalguide to shooting animation.
    1. Animation (Cinematography) –
  Amateurs' manuals
  I. Title
  778.5'347   TR897.5

ISBN 0–240–50973–0

Text set in 10/12 pt Photon Univers, printed by photolithography, and bound in Great Britain at The Pitman Press, Bath

Contents

What is Animation ?

Animation is a way of creating an illusion; it gives life to the inanimate whether real, *common or garden* objects, specially
designed puppets or just drawings. It is a powerful tool for film
making in general. Any shot which cannot be accomplished by
conventional cinematography at a constant camera speed or
would be too expensive or too dangerous will inevitably require
some form of animation. This is so even when the desired effect is
a purely realistic one. Making cartoon films is only one aspect of
film animation although it is probably the best known and certainly
most easily recognisable. Much of the animation in normal film
work comes under the heading of tricks or effects. It often
provokes the inevitable question: How did they do that? Other
aspects are quite unnoticed by the audience, and they are perhaps
the most successful.

A fallacy

The sophisticated audiences of today are no longer puzzled by how
animated cartoons are made. They either take them for granted
because they have been around for such a long time, or they simply assume that "every frame is drawn". This is the way animation
was first explained to me and I am sure to many other people as
well. It is no small wonder then that the myth of the colossal
expense, enormous amounts of energy and time required to make
even a short animated film has become so widespread. The result
of this is that most producers are frightened to touch animation
and most amateurs are well and truly petrified.
Of course "drawing every frame" is a complete fallacy. Not even in
the most subtle and sophisticated form of animation can this be
said to be true. What is true however is that every frame is shot

separately, individually like a series of stills which are in perfect registration to each other so that when they run through a projector at a continuous speed the illusion of movement becomes apparent. Often, the subject (drawing) or the camera is moved a suitable distance between frames to create a panning or zooming movement.

This illusion of movement is all the more realistic when the "animated" object appears to move against a background. Therefore there must be no drastic changes in the background, i.e. it should appear as though it was shot at a continuous speed.

Stop-motion

One of the facts of life of continuous shooting is that the camera does not start instantaneously at the correct speed. Therefore the first few frames are usually spoilt. In addition, when the camera is switched off at the end of a take there is no guarantee that it will stop with the shutter at the "closed" position; if it does not, you get an overexposed "flash" frame. Consequently the whole of an animation sequence (even those sections where there is no movement) must be shot in the same way. That is, using the stop motion (single frame shooting) needed for the animated parts.

Even if the "flash" frames of continuous shooting could be cut out the inevitable changes in the exposure of the background would be too distracting and would spoil an otherwise good animation shot. It is essential to have a stop-motion (single frame) facility on your camera for shooting animation; most 8 mm and some 16 mm cameras have this built in as a standard feature. Additionally, some 8 mm cameras are equipped with magnetic shutters which ensure that the camera always stops in the closed position, but it is still advisable to use stop motion to give absolute evenness of exposure.

External stop-motion motors

As we have already seen most 8 mm and 16 mm cameras have built-in stop-motion facility. However the lack of accurate and easy to read frame-counters as well as reverse operation leave a lot to be desired on most of these cameras to make them into ideal animation cameras. You may also come across some old cameras with quite good movements but which lack the stop-motion facility. The ideal solution to all these problems is to have an external single frame motor. This usually means extending a drive shaft to the outside of the camera and fitting a suitable motor to it. It is best to have a motor which is already geared down so that its output shaft turns considerably slower than the main motor shaft. This ensures greater accuracy. The motor should be able to run both forward and reverse and you need a provision for varying the speed. A circular cam is fitted to the drive shaft with one section cut off. A micro-switch runs in contact with this cam until the cut off section comes opposite it and then the circuit is broken. To make the motor make one more revolution (and so take the next frame) it is necessary to press a button which overides the micro-switch; once the motor has started the cam presses the micro-switch in until a full rotation is completed, i.e. until the circuit is broken by the cut-off section of the cam. All controls can be built into a separate box: on/off switch, forward/reverse; camera speed (motor speed); single frame button; continuous run switch, and an electronic frame counter (linked to the micro-switch). Before attempting to motorise a camera in this way make sure that the take-up facility works in reverse. This, of course excludes certain types of cameras.

A Simple Example

A pencil is seen lying on the table. After about 2 seconds it begins to roll towards the edge of the table; it pauses there for a while before rolling off the edge.

This shot contains two segments of animation (pencil rolling) and three holds — sections where there is no change in the position of the pencil with regard to the table; the first one is at the beginning of the shot before the pencil starts rolling, the second is when the pencil pauses near the edge of the table, and the third is after the

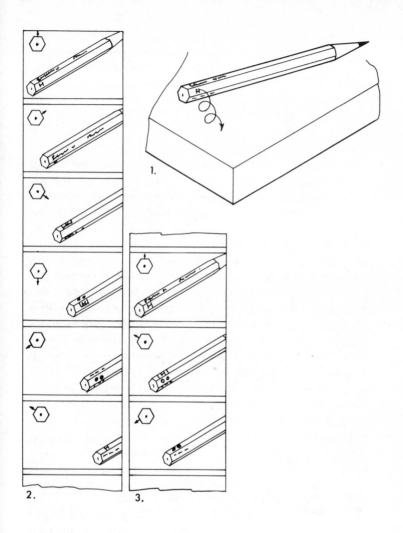

1, A six sided pencil rolling along a table is a simple start for animation. 2, Rotated one facet per frame the pencil appears to roll smoothly along. 3, If the pencil is now rotated five facets per frame, the apparent rolling motion is opposite to the direction of travel.

pencil has fallen off. Each hold lasts for a specific number of frames depending on the desired effect. They should be shot as repeated single frames in the same way as the animated sections.

Timings

The length of time it takes for the pencil to roll to the end of the table depends on the number of frames in which this action is accomplished; and on the speed (in frames per second) at which the film is projected. It is, of course, imperative to decide on the projection speed at which you are working because all the calculations of timing depend on this. It is advisable to use the same speed you do for normal live-action shooting (sound). This allows you to combine your animation shots with other material.

Most pencils happen conveniently to be hexagonal (six-sided). Such a pencil will stay static after it has been rolled a certain amount for each frame (without the danger of it rolling back as a circular one might). In addition, the six equal sides of its surface are very useful for making sure that the pencil is moved on (rolled) an equal amount for each frame. It is helpful if the surface of the pencil is textured and/or engraved – this enhances the illusion of rolling, rather than simply sliding along. Take great care that the pencil does not move lengthwise in between frames and that both ends move in a smooth, if not necessarily straight, line.

Rolling the pencil on from one of its six sides to the next for each frame will produce a smooth rolling movement because it is moved in equal increments for each frame. It will take six frames for one full rotation and in that time the pencil will travel a distance equal to its circumference.

At this rate the pencil rolls three times in one second at a projection speed of 18 fr. p.s. This may be a lot faster than you want. To make the pencil appear to roll at a slower speed, you can take (shoot) two frames per every turn instead of one – this will result in the pencil travelling (rolling) at half the previous rate. Shooting four frames for each increment will make it move half as slowly again, although the danger of the rolling motion becoming jerky is greatly increased. So, with six fixed positions of the hexagon, you are restricted to a reasonably fast roll.

On the other hand the apparent rolling action of the pencil can be greatly increased by moving two or more increments per each frame of picture. There are dangers here also which, will be dealt with later more fully. For example, six increments per frame make it appear to slide, not roll, while if it rolled on for five increments for each frame of picture the result is a little strange — the pencil slides quite fast in the correct direction, but it also appears to be rolling slowly in the opposite direction. Moving the pencil for three increments per frame (three sides or half the circumference) gives a flickering impression. And if the pencil is rotated seven increments per frame (one full turn plus one side) it appears to move very fast in the correct direction but again in a sliding motion while rotating at a much slower rate in the same direction.

Flat Artwork Animation

Flat artwork animation is essentially animation of two-dimensional subjects, i.e., drawings, paintings, photographs, etc. There are three different approaches to flat artwork animation: metamorphosis, paper cut-out animation, and cel animation. They are distinguished in the main by the materials used.

Metamorphosis

In its simplest form this can mean taking a piece of clean paper, pointing a camera at it and taking a few frames at a time to record the different stages of a drawing or painting as it is being done. On projection at normal speed this of course gives the illusion of a piece of artwork materialising from nowhere on the piece of paper. One use is in titling: the first thing to appear on the paper could be the title which is then progressively obscured.

With 16 mm cameras using double-perforated stock (sprocket holes on both sides) you can shoot the action with the artwork upside-down; so that when you run the film in the projector the right way up it appears that a picture has disintegrated into nothing, or at a certain stage a title or new picture is revealed.

In fact there is no need to use paper at all. You can draw on a blackboard, or some other hard material, with chalks or crayons. This allows you to produce disintegration effects by rubbing out parts of the picture progressively between shots.

Registration

For the metamorphosis to work effectively it is essential that each successive frame in the camera is in as near perfect registration to the preceding one as possible. So, the camera mechanism must register the film accurately and, the relationship between the camera and the artwork must be absolutely rigid.

If both the artwork and the camera are firmly supported on solid bases registration is not difficult to achieve. All one has to worry about now is that the artwork itself remains exactly in the same place on its support (i.e. in register) during animation. Those sections of the picture which are not undergoing transformation must always appear the same on every frame until they themselves are transformed. This is easy when the metamorphosis is taking place on one piece of paper where one set of shapes are gradually being painted-over and replaced with other shapes. It is a different matter when a shape (a subject) is required to move across the screen. With a single fixed sheet of paper, you would have to rub out the entire picture after it had been photographed and draw another one slightly farther on, with the appropriate changes in the shape. This is obviously not practical.

Paper animation

Suppose you want a figure to move across the frame. You need a series of drawings that are all slightly different from one another in their outline as well as the relative position in the screen area. You can draw each one on a different piece of paper and then photograph them in succession. Obviously this requires some form of registration between the different pieces of paper so that each consecutive sheet goes in exactly the right place. This is essential to create the illusion of a continuous movement.

You can mark the edges of each piece of paper in a standard way; and then use the marks for lining up the paper at both the drawing stage and shooting stage. However, a far more efficient way is to punch the paper on one edge with a standard paper puncher. You then fit two pins (corresponding in thickness and distances from each other to the pins in the puncher) into the table which will be used to support the artwork during photography. The pins ensure perfect registration of the artwork (on punched paper).

The number of drawings required depends on the extent and kind of movement the figure is supposed to make. You can photograph the artwork at anything from one to five frames per drawing, depending on the desired speed of action and the number of drawings available. Because of a certain appearance of "liquidity" which is characteristic in this type of animation it is advisable to always shoot at a standard number of frames per drawing. This makes for a regular if liquid movement which has a charm of its own. There is a slight change of shape from one drawing to the next in the "static" parts of the drawing because it is done free hand. Any line redrawn several times appears wobbly and liquid.

Problems arise when shooting *holds* with this type of animation. Suppose the character were to pause in the middle of the screen before carrying on with this movement. The appropriate drawing could simply be photographed for the required number of frames. However, on projection, this "hold" would then appear as a freeze when all the liquidity of the scene suddenly disappears. It is possible to get around this by making one or two duplicates of the drawing which is to be held static and alternating these drawings during the hold at the same rate of frames-per-drawing as in the movements.

Adding backgrounds

Paper animation is a quite effective and useful form of simple animation when there are only one or two figures in vision and the background is non-existent or at best a few squiggles at the bottom of the picture. When you need a more definite background, the task of preparing the artwork is that much harder; the background has to be copied on each successive drawing even when it does not change throughout the scene.

If you can paint the background once only, then it is justifiable to spend some time over it and make it a really good, detailed picture. To use the same background for an animated sequence, you must then *cut out* individual drawing of your animated characters and put each one in the right place on the background.

1, With the use of single frame shooting, a title caption or a complete drawing can be built up. 2, You can do more subtle transformations by rubbing out some of the elements as others are added on. 3, Even a brick wall can make a very useful background. If live action is incorporated in this type of shot, the single frame exposure must be compatible with the exposure at continuous running. 4, A finished drawing can be destroyed or transformed into another shape simply by adding more details to it.

Instead of a series of paper drawings depicting the various positions and movements of our character you now have cut-outs of the drawings themselves only. The background can now be firmly fixed to the shooting table and the cut outs placed on it in succession in the same way as before and photographed. You put a platten – a piece of clear glass – over the artwork to keep the cutouts flat and in contact with the background; in addition crinkled tissue paper under the background (which is painted on a flexible cartridge paper) ensures even pressure on the cutout from underneath (see p. 29).

Registering cutouts

In cutting out your drawings from the paper, you have lost the means by which those drawings were registered to each other. You need a new method for registering the cutouts. Take a sheet of backing paper and draw the outlines of the cutout figures for each successive position. Punch this guide and place it over the registration pins. The cutout figure can then be lined up to it accurately for each position (move). Alternatively the animator uses certain details on the background as reference points and animates the cutout to these. In either case it is useful to stick a couple of tiny pieces of double-sided tape behind each cutout. This helps to keep the cutout in position when the glass is lifted off but it must not stick so hard to the background as to leave a mark on it when it is later moved.

The picture quality is better than that from ordinary paper animation because now there is a good quality permanent background. The liquid effect has been removed from that part of the picture. However, the quality of animation has not improved much as far as the character is concerned because the cutouts are still the very same drawings as before.

If your particular subject is to be treated as cutout animation from the beginning, then further improvements are possible. In our example of the clown on a monocycle, the upper part of the figure does not change – therefore only one drawing is necessary. This

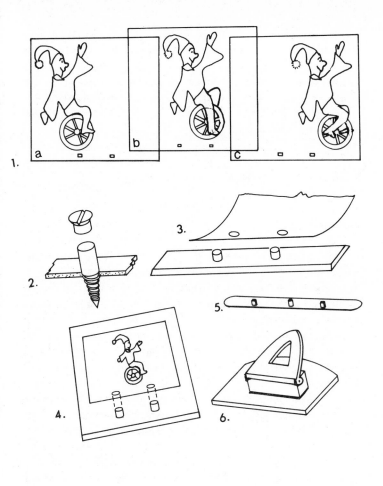

1, A series of drawings can be made to lie in the right place with a registration system. Construction of a simple pegbar. 2, Cut-off wood screws make simple pins. 3, Two pins hold securely. 4, Each successive drawing is registered on the same pins. 5, A loose 3-pin professional pegbar can be used with ready-punched paper of cels. 6, An office punch is fine for preparing materials for a home-made register system.

leaves only the lower part (legs and the wheel) to be treated in much the same way as before. A convenient line is chosen as the "join" between the two sections of the figure and the upper part is cut out slightly bigger at this point to allow for an overlap. This produces two distinct advantages: one, fewer drawings are required and two, the figure can be "bent" at the join thus further enhancing the illusion.

Cutting up the cutouts

A cutout figure can be dismembered completely to give a greater amount of flexibility in the animation of that character. However it is wiser not to have too many pieces unless they are necessary. To animate an arm bending, for example, you may find it more effective to substitute different cut outs than to use a two-part arm.

You can replace the entire arm by one which is drawn slightly bent at the elbow. The substitution method is absolutely essential when it comes to the animation of a head turning from profile to full face. Usually several *in-between* positions are needed to slow down the turn. This also applies to the torso. A "mix" can also be used very effectively to link the two extreme positions without the aid of "in-betweens" (see Mix dissolves).

It is wisest to consider carefully at the outset what kind of movement you want your character to make, so that all the component parts can be prepared facing in all necessary directions before you start shooting. Once you have done that, you can use the same character in a variety of situations and over a variety of backgrounds — provided of course they are drawn in suitable scale and perspective.

Using existing material

Cutout animation is particularly suitable for those who are not too good at doing their own drawing and painting and do not have a friend who could complement this lack of artistic ability. A photograph can be cut out just like a drawing and animated. You can use a magazine picture or one specially printed for your purpose. The mouth can be cut out and moved up and down in synchronisation to a speech or just noise. For more ambitious projects, you might take a series of original photographs of a person's head with different positions of the mouth and jaw (preferably exagerated). You can cut out these heads and animate them in conjunction with a picture of an animal body – or anything else for that matter. When you work with photographic cutouts it is important that they are all printed and processed in the same way so that there is no noticeable change in density from one picture to the next.

Several different kinds of cutouts can be used simultaneously over a simple nebulous background. This is particularly suitable for zany, crazy-comedy animation, where all conventions of logic and perspective are ignored.

Photomation

At its most extreme this is a technique for shooting a live action scene on a still camera and then re-creating it by stop-motion photography. As such, it is hardly of any use at all and is, naturally, seldom tried. A series of photographs can be used in a sequence as freezes of some aspects of an action, producing a rather jerky animation which can be quite effective with certain subjects. The background can be a colour photograph while the cut-out characters are all black and white (or vice versa). This can be done either by tinting the photographs or printing from colour negatives. Simple scenes can be animated from two or more copies of the same picture. For example, with two picture postcards you can make the ship in the bay float away. Cut out the ship from one card and retouch the other to obscure its ship altogether. Place the cutout of the ship in the position where its twin has been painted out on the other postcard and the composite looks exactly the same as it did in the original – with one major difference: now the ship can be made to float across the picture.

Titling

This sort of cut-out animation is one way of producing titles for your travel movies. You can take suitable stills — townscapes, views, hotel rooms, and so on. Then you can introduce the title. For example, you might choose a suitable vista, and bring on a road sign with the right name on it. If you have a lot of patience in the darkroom, you can make a series of pictures of increasing size. So your signpost not only slides in from one side, but also grows (or recedes).

Silhouette animation

The cutouts are prepared in much the same way for silhouette animation as for normal top-lit type, except that thin card is better than paper. The cutouts are painted black and they must be opaque. You do the animation on a light-box by moving the various parts of the character. Although it is quite possible to substitute parts of the figures, you need do that only for the changes of profiles; because the joins are completely invisible!

Some really beautiful results can be obtained with this method but you have to be sure that the subject you have chosen is suitable for treatment in silhouette. Conventional backgrounds are not possible because the figure has to be shown off against a clear area, but they can always be suggested with silhouette shapes.

Cel animation

For the more sophisticated type of animation it is necessary to use acetate cels. Acetate is a clear material which can be obtained in various sizes, either punched or unpunched. The animation is first prepared in outline on punched paper. These outlines are then traced onto the acetate cels using a chinagraph or audiovisual pencil. The animated character is then painted in acrylic paints. Usually on the reverse side of the picture; but highlights or details

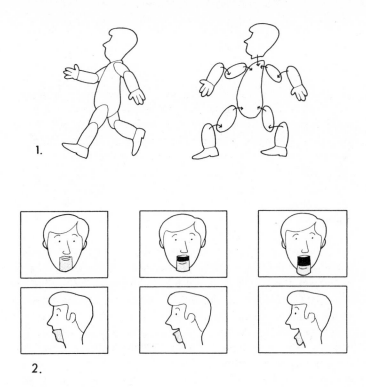

1, Breakdown of a cutout character. Each component can be moved independently or substituted by an alternative one. 2, The character's mouth or jaw can be cut out and moved in sync with a voice.

can be added on top. The background is clearly visible through the unpainted areas of the cel.

The image is held in perfect registration to the background because the cel is punched and placed over the registration pins or a conventional animation pegbar. The character can be broken up and painted on several different cells which are then placed over each other in layers to create the complete image. This means that one of its elements can be changed (animated) quite independently of all others. This obviously results in a greater flexibility of animation.

Registration

Because the cels can be bought already punched to the standard three-pin punch, it may not be necessary to use the two-pin paper punch method. Loose three-pin pegbars are available at reasonable cost. You can just stick one of these pegbars down to your shooting table and register the artwork to it.

It is necessary also to register the background to this pegbar. The simplest way is to acquire a long strip of 35 mm used film and have it punched at intervals. You can make rough cuts at the bottom of the background where the registration holes should be and stick the punched strip of film underneath. If you can, get some ordinary layout paper punched at the same time, for the preparation of rough drawings.

Platten and padding

The cel layers must be absolutely flat on one another, otherwise they may throw shadows. For this you use a piece of clear glass (platten) to press down over the artwork. The weight of the glass is normally sufficient pressure. In fact, excessive pressure can create the appearance of Newton's rings. The background should only be registered on one side and must not be taped down to the table on the other sides — this allows it to breath freely when the platten is raised. If the platten is placed always in the same way and there is no noticeable change in pressure the background will always lie in the same way.

In addition it is normally necessary to put crinkled tissue paper or some other soft material underneath the background to ensure that the cells are in good contact with the background and any unevenness in the background is smoothed out.

Preparing the backgrounds

Prepare the backgrounds on flexible cartridge paper which has been stretched previously to prevent it from crinkling up. The finished background must be free of any crinkles and as flat as possible, particularly when cells are to be used over it.

Stretch the background paper by sticking a slightly larger piece of cartridge paper than you need to a flat wooden board using a wide tape. Sponge it with clean water until it is thoroughly wet. When it is dry again and no crinkles have appeared it is then ready for painting.

Mark the position of the registration holes from the layout paper so that the background can be registered with a punched strip of film. Trace the background layout onto the paper with the aid of a carbon stencil. Water colour paints are normally used on the backgrounds but if necessary you can employ acrylic ones also. When the painting is complete, leave it to dry. Only when it is fully dry can you take it from the painting board; this is done by cutting round the edges of tape with a scalpel.

Multiple backgrounds

Sometimes you have to prepare your background as two drawings so that a cel can be sandwiched between them, as in the case of a window shot. To keep overall evenness you must use a full size background paper even though only a tiny area is actually painted. The window itself should be painted on cel.

Sometimes a detail from the background may have to be transferred onto a cell to enable the characters to go behind it. Often certain foreground details are not painted on the background at all but are separated onto a cell at the outset so that they can be moved about, knocked down, burnt, and generally interfered with while the rest of the background remains unaltered.

Preparation of artwork for cel animation

The layout is a sketch of the composite scene at a key point in animation so that the scale and position of figures relative to the background can be established. It also gives a general impression of what the scene is meant to represent. You prepare a detailed background layout from this, and paint the background as described earlier.

The key positions of the character for this specific scene are then drawn on punched layout paper in registrations to the layout of the background. For these, you must consider such things as size and perspective.

In-betweening is necessary for many movements. When you have finalised the key positions and cleaned them up, you can prepare the in-between positions on punched layout paper. They are suitable intermediate stages in the movement. The number depends on how fast the action is to be and on the number of frames for which each cel is going to be photographed.

Tracing the outlines of the animated character onto acetate cels (in registration) is the next stage. It is done with audiovisual pencil or ink – ideally over a light-box. It is important to use cotton gloves whenever you handle cels both in the preparation of the artwork and in shooting.

Painting the cels comes next. You colour them on the reverse side with acrylic paints. (Other types of paints tend to chip off when the cels are handled later.) The painting should be even and opaque, and this too is easiest done on a light box.

The paper layouts should be numbered and identified in a clear

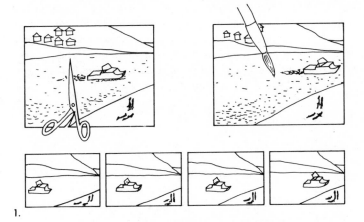

1.

2.

1, Two identical pictures (or postcards) can be used to produce an animated movement of a suitable subject within the picture.

2, The background can be "suggested" in silhouette animation.

way. Transfer these numberings onto the cels as you prepare them. When all the artwork is dry and ready for the camera it is advisable to do a thorough check to make sure that nothing has been left out and that all the elements fit together. Minor faults can be corrected at this stage. If you discover a major fault then it is just as well you found it before you started shooting.

Charting (dope sheet)

A dope sheet is a chart which is made out during the early stages of artwork preparation. In its simplest form it is a breakdown showing the order in which the cels will be assembled on the shooting table against the corresponding frames of picture.

The first section has the numbers printed on it which represent the frames of picture starting with zero. The next section is identified BG and will carry the identification number of the background to be used; if this background is to be substituted by another one at a certain point during the shot, then identify the new background against the appropriate frame where the change takes place. After the background, there are sections for each cel identified by numbers, 1, 2, 3, and 4. It is not advisable to use more than four layers of cel at one time, and you should maintain the same number of cel layers through a shot to avoid any change in density. This may necessitate the use of blank cels.

Animation cycles

Before setting out to do any actual work on an animated sequence it is important to consider the task ahead very carefully. There are a lot of ways in which economies can be made. More often than not, these also result in a much smoother animation. Cycling is probably one of the most important of these economies.

Any form of repetitiveness in the action should be exploited. The same key positions are used over and over again. The number of

In cel animation you can change just part of the picture. The background and the basic cel of the face remain the same. Other features, on separate cels, can be used in different combinations to give different expressions to the character.

33

drawings required depends on the type of action and the desired speed; this again can be varied by the number of frames each drawing is photographed. With the same limited number of drawings the action of a wheel turning can be made to animate indefinitely, with the turning speed changing as required or even slowing down to a hold (see page 14).

Where the last drawing is followed by the first and so on, the cycle is said to be "circular". But this is not an essential feature. In the case of a boy beating a drum, the cycle can start with the hand in the upper position and end at the lower position where the stick is in contact with the drum; at this point a hold of several frames may be included as part of the cycle. The cycle then continues backwards through the drawings to the start, where a further hold may also be appropriate before the cycle continues. Furthermore, the speed at which the arm moves down to hit the drum may be faster than the speed at which it moves back to the start position. You achieve that simply by manipulating the number of frames each of the in-between drawings is photographed (some can be skipped altogether if so desired).

Perhaps the most popular cycles are those of a figure walking. Of course, the leg movements are part of the cycle, but so are the movements of the arms. The head, being a separate drawing, can be animated quite independently. If you have the means of moving a background the correct amount in the opposite direction to the one the character is facing, then you can create the illusion of an animated character walking with just a limited number of drawings in a walking cycle.

In the case of cutouts, the character can walk across the frame with the background static still using only the walking cycle and actually moving the figure forward by the required amount (this is best judged by the size of the step he takes). However, when it comes to cels, they themselves (and consequently the registration pins or pegbar) have to be moved if the background is static.

This problem would also apply to our clown on a monocycle; the leg movements fall very easily into a cycling pattern but the illusion of movement is complete only if either the background or the clown (or both) are moved across the screen.

Cel animation. Composite picture and breakdown of cel layers and background. Note that the tree is copied on an upper cel to enable the character to appear from behind it.

Preliminary fairings

In nature, few objects start moving immediately at their normal constant speed. There is a period of transition from static to full speed during which time the object is developing its velocity, i.e. speeding up. A car which may eventually be running at 60 m.p.h. will take quite a few seconds to reach this speed from a stationary (static) position. Therefore, when animating a car, we have to observe the same rule. Suppose, at a suitable speed, the car takes approximately three seconds to travel 25 cm from point A to point B on the background. The constant speed is simply 25 cm divided by 50 frames (at 18 f.p.s.); i.e. 5 mm per frame. When you start animating the car you will not make it move at this constant speed right away from a static position because this would appear unnatural. A suitable speeding-up rate could be, say – at frame

$$1 = 1 \text{ mm}$$
$$2 = 2 \text{ mm}$$
$$3 = 3 \text{ mm}$$
$$4 = 4 \text{ mm}$$
$$5 = 5 \text{ mm (constant)}$$
$$6 = 5 \text{ mm etc.}$$

(Note that we have shortened the time very slightly – by 4 frames – to make the calculations possible. Always do that if possible.)

In the first four frames we have moved a total of 10 mm which at constant speed of 5 mm represents 2 frames, therefore the fairing-in will make the total animation for the car movement 2 frames longer. The fairing rule applies in reverse also; an object does not stop dead even when it hits a brick wall. If the same progression as above is used in reverse so that the car comes to a halt at position B, the total shot will have been extended by 2 more frames making a total of 54 frames – which is precisely 3 secs at 18 f.p.s.

It is possible to make the speeding up and slowing out appear even slower by using the same speeding increments for 2 frames at a time. This further extends the move in time.

It is possible to start a shot with the animation already moving at constant speed (or continually varying speed) provided it is used as a straight cut. This is just the same as cutting to a live action shot

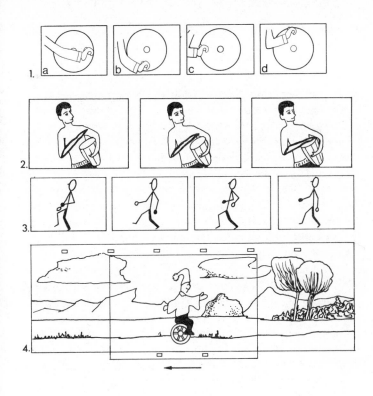

Cycles can reduce the amount of drawing needed for a repetitive action. 1, Key positions for an arm turning a wheel. 2, Key positions for a hand beating a drum. 3, Key positions for walking. 4, A static cycling figure can remain in the centre of the frame as background is moved.

of a car which is already moving at full speed. You need the fairings when the object to be animated is starting to move from a standing position, coming to a stop, or making a dramatic speed change. You need fairings not only for the movement of the entire object, but also various parts of that object. Raising a character's arm in one second may not simply be a matter of dividing the distance by 18 frames (or 9 if shooting on 2 frames). This division is a helpful guide so that you know the kind of increments that are required to be made by the arm in the given number of frames, but the speeding up (fairing in) at the start of the move and slowing out at the end of it must not be overlooked. Sometimes the slowing out can begin as soon as the speeding up has finished without more than one or two frames of "constant" speed. Equally, the fairing can continue through the shot. The shape of the speed-up and slow-out curves determines the flow of the animated movement.

When it is difficult to incorporate the fairing into the artwork itself then the camera can be used to help out. In the above example of the arm being lifted in one second (18 frames) it is possible to divide the distance from the first position to the second by 9. This results in 8 in between drawings (or positions) at equal distance from each other. The speeding up and slowing out effect can be created by shooting the drawing for different times, say:

$$1 = 3 \text{ frames}$$
$$2 = 3 \text{ frames}$$
$$3 = 2 \text{ frames}$$
$$4 = 1 \text{ frame}$$
$$5 = 1 \text{ frame}$$
$$6 = 2 \text{ frames}$$
$$7 = 3 \text{ frames}$$
$$8 = 3 \text{ frames}$$

Total   18 frames

Using the camera to create the fairing effect is particularly useful when working with animation cycles as this eliminates the need for any additional faired drawings. There could also be the cases where this is the only way in which the fairings can be done. If we take our early example of a six-sided pencil rolling across the table we are restricted to one face or facet per turn (i.e. 1/6th of a turn). It cannot be slowed out before it stops by rotating it less than the amount it is being rotated already. Therefore the slow out can only be accomplished by shooting progressively more and more frames for each successive turn. However it is not advisable to exceed 4 frames per move as the juddering effect becomes more pronounced.

Animation of Solid Objects

In its simplest form the animation of three-dimensional objects is very much like flat artwork animation where images are painted one on top of another and all on the same background. For example, a series of buttons of various sizes and colours can be used to form an abstract image or even a recognisable shape. This shape can undergo metamorphosis as the buttons are re-arranged little by little with the camera taking one or more frames for each arrangement. Some buttons can be taken off altogether and others added; they can re-arrange to form the lettering for a title sequence or the lettering can become transformed into a shape. This shape may even resemble a character and can be made to move around the screen area.

If beads are arranged to form the outlines of a face, then by careful re-arranging of the rows forming the features, it is possible to make the face change expression while the basic outline remains the same. All sorts of other materials can be used for this type of animation: sweets of all shapes and sizes, rings and other jewellery, nuts and bolts, even nails and pins. Any kind of shape simply animated in time with music can be very amusing to watch. Metal objects like nails and pins can be animated with the use of a magnet underneath the surface on which they are lying; metal filings are particularly interesting when handled in this way.

Animated lettering

Lettering forms an important part of most title sequences. One way to brighten up your titles is to animate them. You can use letters cut-out, moulded or bent from suitable materials.

With care and careful substitution, you can make your title emerge from a sea of swirling letters, then merge again to form a new word. One interesting idea is to have the letters metamorphose one to another. You need a flexible medium – such as pipe cleaners or plasticine. Make the letters from them, then transform them bit by bit to another letter. Shoot a suitable number of frames at each stage.

Don't start with anything too elaborate, though. You must ensure that the static parts of each sequence remain entirely unmoved between shots – unless you want the words to dance irregularly before your audience's eyes. There is more detail on p. 174.

Adding the background

As animation of a series of small objects is normally photographed on a flat surface, this can be simply a plain one-tone background or it can be a drawing or a photograph. It can be an abstract or a realistic image; it could even be a photograph of a specific arrangement of beads, buttons or letters over which the same objects are now animated. The animated shapes made up in this way can be used to appear as part of the picture which is used in the background although difficulties with shadows tend to destroy this illusion. However, if the effect is worth the trouble then you can use a piece of clear glass placed a few inches above the background and animate your beads on it. (See the section on lighting, page 134.)

There is of course no reason why some of these shapes cannot be shot against real backgrounds like a series of beads snaking their way through the grass or a dozen door-handles marching across the street (if you can persuade police to hold up the traffic for a few hours).

Puppets

If you string up a few beads, buttons or jellytots on a flexible wire such as a pipe-cleaner, you can make a puppet figure which can then be animated in front of various kinds of backgrounds. The animation is done in much the same way as the animation of cut-outs. The problem of registration manifests itself here in the need for stability; the figure has to be able to maintain its overall shape while only one part of it is being animated. This can be a particularly great problem when it comes to walking, especially where the figure has only two legs. Fortunately most puppets, even the most sophisticated ones, are a form of caricature of real life figures. So making the feet extra big does not immediately make the viewer conscious of the stability problem which may have forced the evolution of that particular shape.

Toys as animation puppets

There are a lot of very well made toys on the market. They can make excellent subjects for animation. Some of them can be used as they are and others may need a little modification to make them more flexible or to improve their balance. Mechanical toys such as cars and trains are such good replicas of the real thing that it would be hard to make anything better for this purpose. With press-together building blocks, it is possible to make strange geometric figures and even entire sets.

Though you are not restricted to specially constructed toys, you can animate virtually any object, papier-mache figures ... modelling clay ... even pots and pans ... jam jars (with or without faces painted on them) ... all of these offer great possibilities. *Objects trouvé*, such as a rock from the garden or a broken branch can be helped along with a bit of paint to bring out the likeness to a figure which their shape suggests. Origami figures are also very useful particularly if the animation shows how a single sheet of paper takes on various shapes.

Structure of a puppet

Simple shapes and bendy toys are good starting points, but you may sometimes want something more sophisticated.

A good animation puppet is built around a firm metal skeleton which is jointed to give all possible moves that may be required.

Toys as animation puppets. Jointed construction blocks can be used to make puppet figures. The best way is to look at children's toys as they play with them. That should give you ideas for your animation.

Some of these joins are detachable so that replacement limbs, heads etc. can be used; this way the same basic puppet can be a girl with one head and a girl's costume and a boy with another head and costume. The stability, which is all important is built into the design of the skeleton and the feet can be made heavier than the rest of the structure.

The basic skeleton is covered in rubber (as are the detachable parts) and the real shape of the puppet is created at this stage, although a fat man and a skinny one may in fact be built around exactly the same type of skeleton.

With careful animation, based on close observation of movements and mannerisms of people and animals, these puppets can take on an appearance of real living things — much more so than in the case of string puppets. In larger puppets, the facial features can be animated; but this should be reserved for close-ups. Ideally one should have a larger version of the key puppets' heads for this. Lip movements are particularly difficult to accomplish for synchronised dialogue and it is best to rely on body movements combined with changes of expression to convey the emotion with or without dialogue.

Changes of expression are best accomplished by substitution: the head with the sad face is simply taken off and another one with a happy face put in its place. Inevitably, this is best done off screen. However, with care, it can be done in vision if accompanied with a "natural" movement of the head which is taken through several frames to cover up any misregistration. You may also need a couple of in-between heads. Alternatively a mix (dissolve) from one head to the next can be very effective. Substitution is particularly useful for the hands. Instead of animating the puppet's hand to take hold of an object — the hand itself is substituted at the appropriate moment for the one which is already holding that object. (or its substitute).

Some animators have gone to the extreme of designing puppets which have no mouths and hardly any prominent facial features so that their blank expression can suit any kind of situation; so eliminating the need for the substitution of heads altogether. Their appeal is a matter of personal taste.

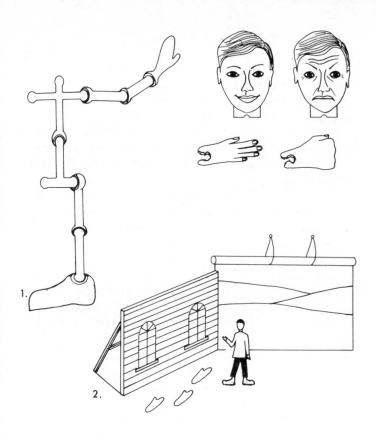

1, Basic structure of a very well made puppet with interchangeable heads and hands. Note that the parts clip together firmly, and the feet must be big and heavy. 2, Simple puppet set, using one flat and a backdrop (footprints in the sand).

Background sets

Puppets can, of course, be animated in front of painted or photographic backgrounds. These are really best used as backdrops representing distant background. Middle ground and foreground have to be constructed as little solid models. Take care in the design and construction of these sets to allow enough room to make action area accessible to the animator. Think, too, of the positioning of lights at this stage (see page 136). Since these sets can be used for a number of shots and from various angles, it is justifiable to spend a lot of time on their construction (unlike a two dimensional background which can't be re-used as much because it represents the view of a scene from one angle only).

At its best, a puppet set is a film set in miniature and the trouble taken in making it is always well worth it.

Because puppets are basically stylised representations of real beings they also blend in very well with purely stylised backgrounds. However, it is wise to have enough of a set there, however abstract, to give depth and perspective to the picture.

Dynamation

This is a term frequently used to describe the very realistic looking animation of extremely well made puppets which are combined with live action to add to the illusion of a real living creature. They are usually prehistoric of fantasy creatures like dinosaurs, King Kong, etc. The technique is exactly the same as normal puppet animation except that it is done to absolute painstaking perfection using realistic backgrounds. Commonly these are front-projected or back-projected so that the puppet appears to be actually in the background picture. Various other techniques available to the professional film maker help to make the illusion of realism even more convincing. However there is a lot that a determined enthusiast can achieve in this area. (See pages 205 and 211.)

Whatever you animate, you need the same calculations on timing and movements. The fairings we discused under flat artwork are just as important with models or puppets.

Cut-out puppets

Puppets are normally solid objects which can be photographed from any side because of their round shape. A cut-out puppet is really only a flat drawing cut out from a reasonably thick card which is then fixed in an upright position and photographed as a solid object in a set instead of a flat drawing. The main problem with such a puppet is of course that it must always be positioned with its flat side facing the camera otherwise the outline and the drawing appear distorted. This type of puppets can be used entirely on their own, but because the movement is very restricted they are best suited for use as secondary characters while the main action revolves around a full solid puppet. This way a lot of time and effort can be saved in the preparation of the puppets.

Animating the cut-out puppets

Obviously the movement of the cut-out puppets is very restricted. Apart from sliding in any direction (but always facing the camera) no other movements can be done very easily. If a more solid base is used (such as thin plywood) and cut to the outlines of the drawing then the drawing itself can be attached to this base. This would allow for a certain amount of cutting up of the figure to be done, e.g. the head can be a separate drawing which can be substituted for another one with a different expression while the rest of the puppet remained unaltered. This clearly opens up a number of new possibilities but we are still limited by the outline of the drawing. If on the other hand the base support is cut out smaller than the drawing then a certain amount of side to side movement of the head and limbs will be possible. In some cases the base support can consist of a wooden stick supported in a wooden block. Substitution of certain parts of the figure and a certain amount of independent movement of these parts or the whole figure forms the basis for animating the cut-out puppets. In cases where drastic alterations in shape of the cutout are required then the entire cutout is substituted.

Using live characters as puppets

A live character can be made to perform impossible feats with the use of animation. Before attempting this form of animation it is absolutely essential to ensure that there is no other movement of any kind within the frame, such as tree branches blowing in the wind and people or vehicles moving in the background. A person can appear to slide effortlessly along the grass by simply taking one frame at each of a number of positions; the speed at which he moves will depend on the distance he moves in between each frame. For best results the person should move an equal amount between each frame otherwise the sliding effect will appear jerky. In fact all other rules regarding animation apply equally.

The posture of the figure should remain unaltered – and this can be very difficult with a real person. A secondary movement of the figure can be helpful in hiding any discrepancies, i.e. the person can rotate (spin) gradually while he is sliding. Incidentally if this effect is attempted on sand then the figure can leave a "plough" tracing on the sand with their feet and this can be used to inscribe a title.

Another useful application of this technique is to make people wiggle out or pop out of holes or crevices, or disappear into them.

Movement in Flat Artwork Animation

The stand

So far in dealing with the various forms of flat artwork animation we have assumed that the artwork is simply placed on a shooting table. A camera designed to take single frames is then suspended over this artwork by some means or other. At its most basic the shooting table can in fact be an ordinary table. It should, though, be of rigid construction. With registration pins fixed into the surface, you can put the artwork directly onto this table. Place the shooting table next to a wall and that can be used to suspend the camera. The axis of the camera lens has to lie perpendicular to the table surface, and point to the centre of the shooting area.

The shooting area is dictated by the size of the table as much as by anything else. So in most cases the camera lens should point straight down at the centre of the table. To accomplish this, the camera has to be mounted away from the wall. To decide the length of the mounting bracket, subtract the distance between the camera mounting point and the lens axis from the distance to the centre of the table. Construct the bracket from wood or metal, with a metal camera mounting plate. Fix the camera to this plate with a spare screw (tripod adaptor) fitted through a hole in the supporting plate. This is normally sufficiently firm, but you may want additional security against the camera moving during operation. For this, fix an angle made of two thin strips of metal to the mounting plate. You locate two sides of the camera base in the angle to ensure against the camera twisting. The screw hole on the plate should be made a little bigger to allow for the camera to be located firmly against the corner.

The height above the shooting table at which the camera is mounted depends on the type of zoom lens fitted to that camera. It is best to position the camera so that the zoom at its extreme widest position (short focal length end) covers the shooting area of the table; this then makes it possible to use the full range of the zoom during the shooting. Of course you must mount the camera within its focusing distances of the table.

Naturally, wall-mounting makes this sort of arrangement difficult if not impossible to move about (though, indeed, there is seldom need for it to be moved at all). As an alternative, you can build a complete unit in one. It should really be of a much more rigid construction to achieve the necessary stability. It is worthwhile looking around for some useful tool which could be converted to this sort of use. The most obvious is a rigid enlarger. You can sometimes buy old large models at very reasonable prices. One with a tilted column is probably strongest. However, a truly vertical column gives you the chance of moving your camera up and down if necessary. Alternatively, the stand used for supporting a home power drill for vertical drilling operations has both the right shape and the necessary rigidity to recommend it. On either of these, the camera mount can be adjusted up and down to give a choice of working heights. In fact, some of the ready-made animation stands available for use with 8 mm cameras are designed on very much the same lines as the drill stand, but with added refinements. The stand can also be constructed as a box-like shape which makes it relatively more stable but clumsy to operate.

The shadow board

The wall or the supporting column of the stand can be used also to support additional gadgets such as the shadow-board. This at its simplest is a piece of black card with an aperature cut out in it and placed in front of the lens. Its main function is to prevent any scatter light from reaching the lens, and to prevent any reflections (of the camera body and camera mount) in the glass on the table. If it is made slightly more rigid it can be used to carry masks, optical glass, etc. (see shadowboard effects page 167).

Instead of a wall or column mounting, you can suspend the shadow board on two rods from the camera mount. This allows you to make a provision to move the shadow board closer or further away from the lens.

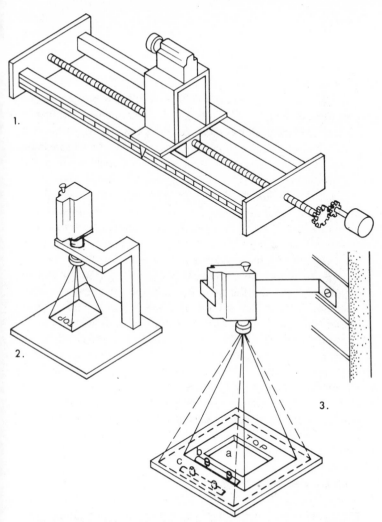

1, Horizontal tracking set up. A tape alongside the track indicates various camera positions, for manual or motorised movements. Counter-balanced, this compact unit can be used at an inclined position between 45° and 90° if needed.

2, Vertical set up.

3, Vertical set up, with backlight cutout (a), may have separate pegbar positions (b, c) for different field sizes.

Platten

As we have already seen in most cases you need to keep artwork absolutely flat. The simplest way is just to put a loose piece of good quality glass down on it; but the tediousness of lifting it off and putting it back in the same position over and over again can be very disheartening. They do say you have to be a bit of a masochist to want to make animation films, but there is a limit even to that. It is much easier to have a simple hinged system. The glass can be mounted in a frame which is then hinged to a wall bracket or the table itself. In either case it should be designed so that it is perfectly parallel to the surface of the table at the point of contact. This is essential to produce even pressure on all areas of the artwork. It is very important that the bottom surface of the platten frame is at the same level as the surface of the glass, otherwise this area will be in contact with the artwork before the glass. As this is not such a simple matter to achieve you can get around it by using a platten which is larger than the table and mounting it in a three-sided frame — the fourth side is the side of the registration pegs and is left free to enable the glass to be in contact with the artwork.

The platten can be spring-loaded. The spring can either reduce the pressure on the artwork, or hold the platten in the upper position. The latter is used when there is a lot of cel animation, and so quick changing is important; the platten is pulled down into position and held during the photography and then released to leave the operator with free hands for changing the cels.

Field sizes

The shooting area is called the field size and is indicated by the horizontal length of the photographed frame area. The animation artwork is normally prepared on standard sizes such as 8 inch or 12 inch (larger sizes than these are used as well). The choice of the size depends on the amount of detail in the picture, as well as whether any enlargement of that picture is needed (by zooming).

Registration pegs

The register pegs can be made out of sawn off wood screws of the same diameter as the paper puncher set at the same distance apart. They can be fitted directly into the table or into a separate strip of wood which then fits into one or more grooves cut into the table. A blank piece of wood of the same size but without pins can be used in the groove when the register pegs need to be moved farther back to accommodate a larger shooting area.

If the table is in a fixed position — and normally it should be — then the first groove will be in the correct position for working on your smallest field size. You move the peg bar back to another groove for the larger size. It is worth remembering that the centre of all field sizes is in the *same* spot on the table.

Instead of cutting grooves, you can make the register pins so that they can be unscrewed from their positions when not required. However, unless the fitting is very well made, the pegs may not always go back to their correct position; and the separate strip idea is better if you want to move them. Another way around the problem is to have the register pegs fixed permanently into a flat board which is completely detachable from the table. You clamp the board on it as dictated by the field size. You can then use the board (off the table) for preparing your artwork.

It is possible to buy a loose pegbar of the type used by the professional animators. The bar consists of three standard pins (one round and two flat) mounted into a thin metal strip. The loose peg bar can be taped down anywhere on the table to give perfect registration (use double-sided tape). This is obviously only justifiable when cels are used in some quantity because they can be bought ready punched to this standard punch.

The register pins can be on any of the four sides of the frame area. It is best to standardise (unless there are special needs). It is most convenient to set them on the side nearest to the operator. If the camera is mounted as described earlier, then the artwork should be placed upside-down on the shooting table in order for it to be the right way up for the camera. You work with the picture upside-down which is something you can get used to although it may be very disconcerting at first. If your pins are nearest you, your registration holes come at the top of the picture. It is important to remember this when preparing the artwork!

When you have a lot of improvising to do under the camera (such as the animation of cutouts) the upside-down position tends to make the work even harder. You can turn the camera the right way up with a support bracket that goes around the camera. It is important to ensure that this kind of bracket does not obscure any of the camera controls and so limit its functions. Inevitably, some cameras are a lot more difficult to mount in this way than others. Don't cut out holes in the bracket if you can avoid it. They make the bracket weaker and more prone to vibration.

Backlight

Backlighting is a useful asset in flat artwork animation. For this, you can cut out the central area of the table. The sides of the cut-out area are grooved so that when a piece of clear glass is placed in it, its upper surface lies in the same plane as the table surface. This way it does not interfere with normal top-light shooting. Because the size of the cut-out area is limited by the register pins for the smaller field size, you may find it easier to make a separate light box. You place that on the table when you want back-light shooting. The obvious advantage of this is that because it is mobile the same lightbox can be used for the preparation of artwork. There are disadvantages to this also which we discuss in the lighting chapter (see page 133).

Horizontal set up

Flat artwork animation is most conveniently shot on an animation stand of a vertical construction. However, quite a lot of this kind of work can be done on a horizontal set up which is easier to construct in some ways. Some titling kits can be used both horizontally and vertically.

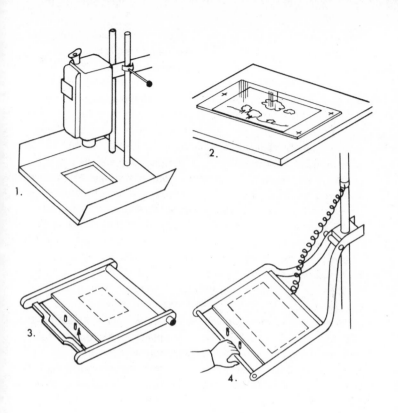

1, An adjustable shadow board prevents the cameras being reflected from the platten. 2, A piece of loose glass may be placed on the artwork. Use some form of register marks to make sure that it is always replaced in the same position. 3, Changing artwork is easier if the pressure glass is mounted as a platten. 4, A spring loaded platten is held down in position for shooting.

The zoom

Zooming is a continuous change of the field size photographed during one shot. Without a zoom lens it is accomplished by moving the camera towards or away from the artwork. The problems of maintaining the same position for the lens centre and sharp focus during the full length of the track calls for the construction of precision machinery of the size, weight and price which can only be justified by professional use.

If you have a means of changing the camera position and therefore the field size you are better advised not to use it for zooming. Your tracking is likely to be anything but perfectly straight and so cause the picture to weave about. Further, the sheer difficulty of making measured movements and counterbalancing the camera is enough to put most people off. The horizontal set up has an advantage here over the vertical one in that it is always easier to find a means of moving the camera horizontally; however the problem of following focus and unevenness of the track remain.

For 8 mm and 16 mm work with animation stands of a simple construction, a zoom lens is the best way of making continuous changes of field size during a shot (zooming). Indeed the zoom lens is often an integral part of an 8 mm camera. The important requirement here is that if the zoom lens is motorised it should have a manual override for animation work.

Focusing

It is a characteristic of a zoom lens that if focused on a subject it keeps the same focus during the full length of the zoom. You always focus at the longest focal length setting. That is the most accurate. In addition it is a good idea to make a wax pencil mark on the lens to indicate the focus position as this is always the same on a fixed set up. Once you have established the focus, you can use a piece of tape to ensure that the focus ring is not moved accidentally when other lens controls are used.

Zoom lens operation

When a fixed focal length lens is moved towards an object, the successive enlargement of the area photographed (zooming in) is very much the same as the eye coming closer to an object. The angle of view of the eye does not change. With a zoom lens, the enlargement of the area seen by the lens is achieved not by coming closer to it but by changing the angle of view from wide to narrow. This can produce unnatural perspective in conventional shooting; but for flat artwork the results are exactly the same as tracking. The third dimension, and therefore the perspective, exists only in the artwork itself. The change in the angle of view of the lens merely alters the field size being photographed. If the zoom lever (or ring) is moved a certain amount for each frame – the result on projection will be a continuous change of field size, i.e. a zoom.

The length of a zoom *in terms of time*, is the number of frames it takes from the start to the end of the zooming action. The length of a zoom is also determined in the extent, or the amount the angle of view of the lens changes from the start to the end of the zooming action. This is usually expressed in terms of the ratio between the field size at the start of the zoom and the linear field size at the end.

Irrespective of the actual focal lengths of the lens at various positions a 2:1 zoom means that one field size is twice as big as the other. In working out the zooms it is best to think in terms of the start field size and the end size only.

When you have chosen the start and end field sizes of a zoom, mark the zoom ring on the lens. You can do it with a wax pencil, but it is better to stick on a strip of white tape. Then you can mark your positions on this tape directly. Take off the tape with extreme positions of the zoom marked up. The distance between the two marks on the tape is physical representation of the extent of the zoom. Now you can divide this by the number of frames the zoom is required to last, i.e. the length of the zoom in time. If it is a constant zoom from start to finish then just divide the distance into equal increments (with a ruler). Put the tape back on the lens (in position) and you can turn the zoom ring from one mark on the tape to the next per frame (or per 2, 3, 4 frames if you wish).

Fairing the zoom

More often than not a zoom is an integral part of a shot (in fact there may be more than one zoom in the same shot). The shot may start with a hold at one field size and the camera then zooms into a detail of the picture. If so, the zooming cannot be done at the same increment throughout. It would appear to start with a jerk. To avoid that, the move has to be faired-in just like an artwork movement (see page 72).

The simplest method is to "project" a semicircle onto the tape. Mark the start and the end positions on the tape as before; put the tape on a large flat surface so that a semicircle can be drawn connecting the two points marked. Divide the circumference of this semicircle by the number of frames the zoom is required to take. Project these points at right angles to the line connecting the two points on the tape. The middle is more or less constant.

The tape is now complete with a graduated speed up and slow out. If you wish, you can extend the constant section by using two quarter circles at each end of a straight line. If the shot is required to cut on a zoom then the fairing-in section is not necessary – you can adjust the tape marks so that the zoom begins with constant increments. As with other movements, you may need to change the length of your zoom slightly to give you simple measurements. This may mean making the zoom a few frames longer or shorter than originally intended. As it is bad practice to cut out of a zooming shot while the zoom is still going (except in special circumstances and mixes) the fairing out is almost always necessary. Shooting on two or more frames per increment for the zoom should be avoided because it tends to show up quite noticeably. This can be a bit of a problem when very long zooms – in time, are required over a short range. To overcome this, you need to lengthen the scale. One way is to attach a semi-circular scale to the side of the camera and use an indicator from the zoom ring.

Another method is to use a strip of metal or card curved in the same way as the lens body. Extend a pointer from the zoom ring and move it on the tape scale as before.

Zoom curves

If you move the zoom ring or lever the same amount for every frame, you change the angle of view of the lens by the same number of degrees at a constant rate. Contrary to expectations, this does not produce a constant change in image size. The zoom lens acts in the same way as the eye. Think of travelling towards a bridge at constant speed on a straight section of road. When you first see it, a long way off, the bridge does not seem to be getting more noticeably bigger; and then as you get nearer it changes in size increasingly quickly, until in the last few hundred yards it looms up at an ever increasing rate. A zoom at constant increments on a photograph of a bridge produces the same effect. This is unfortunate, because in absence of the third dimension, the feeling of realism is spoilt by the distinct impression that the entire picture is coming towards us at an increasing rate.

The increase in the rate of travel is particularly noticeable at large ratios (longer zooms) and at the small field sizes. The increase in the image size follows a logarithmic curve.

It is possible to operate a zoom so that it follows an exponential curve but it is hardly worth the trouble for the majority of normal shooting. It is useful to be aware of the reasons for the effect; an occasional attempt at straightening out a logarithmic curve may be justified. This is most likely to be the case with long zooms, and is achieved by making progressively smaller increments from the wider field sizes (wide angle) to the smaller ones (narrow angle). Any fairings are then added to this curve or pattern of increments.

Moving pegbar

In animation, your camera is fixed in relation to the artwork. So, to achieve movement, you must move the artwork. If the camera is required to pan along a drawing or other artwork from left to right (called East to West in animation terms), this is achieved by moving (panning) the artwork itself in the opposite direction.

The fixed pegbar, described earlier, which is used for registering the artwork on the shooting table can be made to slide in a groove which extends the full length of the table. So the artwork can be panned along in a straight line and still be in correct registration; furthermore, any changes in the artwork (such as when using an animation cycle) will stay in registration while the animation continues. The effect obtained is as though the camera is panning along an animated scene. This illusion is enhanced if there is a constant (unmoving) background to this picture. A set of fixed pegs on the opposite side of the frame area can serve to register this background. If those pegs too can move, then you can move the background in the opposite direction, if you want to.

If you are to pan, your artwork must be large enough to fill the frame at both ends of the move. Cels must be long enough so that the edge of the acetate remains outside the area. Otherwise you will get a line across the picture. Because the artwork has to be longer than the standard size it is sometimes difficult to maintain good registration with only one set of register pegs. The moving pegbars can be made longer so that you can fit two or three sets of pegs to them at regular intervals.

Calibrating the pegbar

A pointer attached to the pegbar can indicate the amount the pegbar is moved between each frame. Make up a scale of the full length of the pan on a tape. Stick it to the shooting table in line with the groove along which the pegbar travels. You can work out fairings and indicate them on this tape in the same way as for the zoom.

Mechanical drives

A pegbar can be moved along in its groove by a variety of

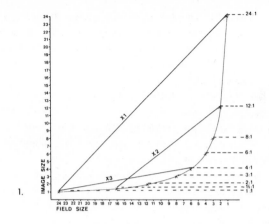

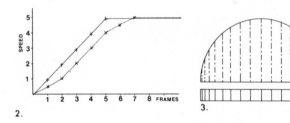

1, As the camera is moved in (or zoomed in) from the widest to the smallest field size in equal increments, the object being photographed increases unequally. Image size varies logarithmically with lens position. When the camera track follows an exponential curve the increase in the image size is constant, e.g. X1 – 24 FS to 1 FS, X2 – 16 FS to 2 FS, X3 – 24 FS to 6 FS.

2, Fairing in moves reduces the abrupt start and finish. Fairing in to constant speed of 5 increments in a total of five units (equivalent to 4 frames at constant speed) 1, 2, 3, 4–5 constant (10 units = 4 frames constant). This could be smoothed out $\frac{1}{2}$, 1, 2, 3, 4, $4\frac{1}{2}$–5 constant (15 units = 6 frames at constant). Similar fairings can be produced at other speed changes. 3, One method of producing a fairing scale: divide a circle into the total number of increments, and 'project' them onto a scale.

mechanical means. The simplest is a worm-screw drive. The screw shaft is supported at each end in bearings. One end has a small wheel and a handle fitted for turning the shaft. An ordinary nut moves up and down the screw as the shaft is rotated – the nut is fixed to the pegbar, which then moves along with it.

You can use a screw on top of the table outside and running parallel to the pegbar, or build it into the table. A built-in screw is less likely to cause obstruction and is much neater in appearance. Instead of a worm-screw, you can use a rack and pinion type of drive for a moving pegbar. The rack runs into a metal groove set into the shooting table. This is more sophisticated but also more difficult to make. It allows the drive wheel (control wheel) to be mounted at right angles to the pegbar and on the front side of the table which makes it easy to operate.

Calibration

Mechanically driven pegbars are easier to calibrate and are therefore more accurate than simple sliding bars. The distance the pegbar is required to move (length of pan) can be calculated by counting the number of full revolutions the wheel has to be turned to reach the desired position. This number is then divided by the number of frames (length of pan in time) to obtain the correct constant increment per frame. In addition the circumference of the wheel can be divided to give fractions of a turn; this is particularly useful for calculating and executing fine speed-ups and slow-outs (fairings) as well as for very slow pans. Purely visual aids such as tape along the pegbar, can still be used with the mechanically driven pegbars. However, you are only likely to need this when the pan is required to follow an unusual curve for speeding up and slowing out. It does, though, give a useful double check on the start and finish positions concerned.

Play in the system can lead to inaccuracies. So, you should always take up any slack by arriving at your final position from the same direction for each frame. If you overshoot the mark, go back past it, and come up to it again.

Counters

A gear placed on the drive shaft can be used to drive a small *mechanical* counter. This way you ensure absolute accuracy (both forward and reverse) because the counter can be made to indicate fractions of a wheel-turn – usually ten units to a full wheel turn. If the distance the pegbar travels during one turn of the wheel is a convenient unit of measure, then each unit on the counter represents a corresponding unit or number of units of real distance the pegbar is moved.

The counter can be directly connected so that it reads a particular number whenever the pegbar is in a certain position. Such a counter is zeroed when it is fitted in. The zero point should be with the pegbar in the central position. More sophisticated counters allow you to reset them to zero at any time. If so, then it can be zeroed at the start position of a pan. Move the pegbar to the end position, and the frame counter then indicates the length of the pan. You divide this by the number of frames (length of pan in time) to give a constant increment per frame.

Electronic counters can be used in place of the mechanical ones. One simple way is to trigger a micro-switch by one or more round-headed screws positioned on the outside of the peg-bar drive control wheel. Each electronic impulse moves the counter by one unit. A single screw counts one for each revolution. Several more "triggers" at regular intervals along the circumference of the wheel lead to the counter representing smaller divisions of the wheel. This enables a finer, more accurate indication of the distance travelled by the pegbar. A more sophisticated electronic counting system uses a transparent disc which is fitted to the shaft. This disc is divided into a required number of divisions which are painted black at regular intervals. A tiny beam of light is directed through the disc painting to a photocell on the other side. As the disc rotates the black areas interupt the beam and the clear areas allow it to reach the photocell and so activate the electronic counter to which it is connected.

The simplest type (and the cheapest) of electronic counters count only forward. So, once the distance of the pan is measured, and the bar moved back to the start, they have to be re-zeroed. So you need auxilliary visual aids; such as marking up start and end points on a tape stuck to the table.

Better electronic counters count both forward and reverse. They can be re-zeroed when required. The accuracy of the electronic counters depends on the trigger mechanism and the micro-switch. On the whole, these can be made to be quite reliable. The biggest advantage of electronic counters is that they can be placed in a convenient position. You can even have them away from the shooting table altogether, built into a little control box. They normally require a 12 v power supply.

Marking the control wheel

During very long pans at constant increments it can become tedious to refer to the counter all the time. The non-stop mental arithmetic, however simple, takes up a considerable amount of the operator's concentration. It can often result in mistakes. For example, at a constant increment of 0.2 of a wheel turn, the operator is adding up: 2, 4, 6, 8, 10; 12, 14, 16, 18, 20; etc. It is easier to divide the circumference of the wheel by 5 and indicate each point as A, B, C, D, E — the operator then just follows this easy succession of letters instead of adding up numbers.

If the constant increment is 0.25 and the control wheel is turning anti-clockwise, the operator would have to subtract 0.25 continually: 7.75, 7.50, 7.25, 6.75, 6.50, 6.25 etc. A tape stuck around the wheel and divided into four units, and marked A, B, C, D, makes this shooting a lot easier. The letters are placed in the direction in which the wheel is turning so that they always read A, B, C, D, etc. Perhaps the most important use of this type of division of the wheel is in the instances where 1/3 of a wheel turn is required. For example, it takes 30 wheel turns to cover the full length of the pan and the pan is 90 frames long; the constant increment is 1/3 of a wheelturn. The numerical division is, of course, a recurring fraction which it is not quite practical to set with the aid of a counter alone. Whereas, dividing the wheel into three

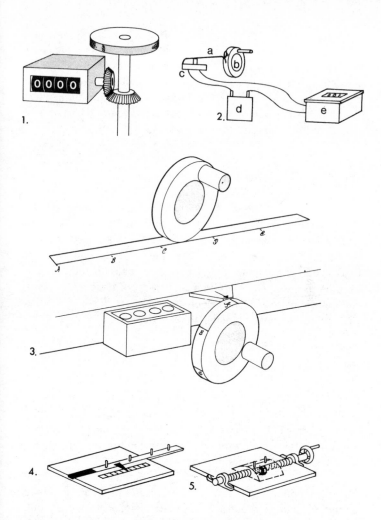

Counting frames and movement. 1, Mechanical counter. 2, Electronic counter. A small lever (a) is pushed up by a head of a screw (b) to activate a micro switch (c) which completes the electric circuit from the battery (d) to the frame counter (e). 3, Tape is used to divide up the pan wheel for mechanical drives. Each segment is identified by a letter. 4, Simple slide and scale movement. 5, A screw-drive made from a threaded rod and a nut.

equal parts is simple. You can ignore the counter unless you want a speed up or slow out. Still, you use the wheel marks for the constant portions of the pan. When you want larger units than one wheelturn, you can still use division of the circumference. For a constant increment of 1.33333 divide the wheel into three equal parts (A, B, C) as before. Then for each move you turn from A to A plus B; B to B plus C; C to C plus A; A to A plus B; and so on.

'Jumping' the pegbar

When the background is extra large the pan can be too long to be accommodated by the full travel of the pegbar. You achieve a continuous pan by jumping the pegbar back to the start position. Stick the background down to the table at the end of the pan. Take the pegs out of the pegbar and slide the bar back to the opposite extreme position. Align it with a second set of registration holes, and put the pegs back in position. Now you can continue the pan with the same constant increment as before.

North-South (vertical) panning

East-West (horizontal) panning along the artwork and backgrounds is probably the most commonly used; but it is often necessary to pan in other directions. It is not practical to build into the same table both East-West and North-South panning pegbars. So the requirement is met in different ways.

The pegbar can be built into an animation board instead of directly into the shooting table. You can then place this board under the camera so that the pegbar runs in any direction that you want. That way, you can do North-South pans (or any other you want to). The only point to remember is that (for a North-South pan) the artwork would have to be pegged to the side instead of top or bottom of the frame (side-pegged). If two parallel pegbars are built into the same animation board, one on each side of the frame, then double moves can be performed in the same way as in the case of the East-West pans. These two moves are not necessarily always in opposite directions – they could be in the same direction but at different speeds; i.e. parachutist in foreground falling slower through the frame than another parachutist who is farther away. (In this case the background would be stuck down between the two pegbars as it is static.)

Diagonal panning

Diagonal panning in any direction is also possible with the type of animation board and moving pegbars described above. It is obviously very important for the artwork to be pegged correctly before this can be done. The artwork is always pegged to the camera horizontal – regardless of the direction of travel. So you have to decide the angle of the pan when preparing the artwork.

Rotation

Changing the angle of the pan of a moving pegbar could be made easier if the entire animation board is mounted on to a device to enable it to be rotated a full 360° around its centre. This can take various forms from a circular groove in the shooting table to a well engineered double ring with ball-bearing runners. A groove in the table is rather crude but it enables the animation table to be positioned at any angle so that any kind of diagonal pan can be performed, and as long as this is all that is expected from it – it is perfectly satisfactory. However with a well engineered rotation ring it is possible to shoot spinning and rotating shots; indeed curved pans are possible with the combined use of the pegbar and rotation. It is most important that the rotation can be "locked" in a chosen position when only the pegbar is used.

If you are prepared to forgo backlighting, you can rotate your animation board on a central bearing, against a calibrated circular scale. An old record turntable (without motor) could provide a suitable base.

The compound

So far we have an animation table with a pegbar (or two) which is positioned on a second flat surface such as a table via rotation device. This still restricts the moves that can be made — most particularly, you cannot do a double move during the same shot. For example, when the shot involves a pan along a certain scene in an East-West direction, and then pan up to reveal a detail which is outside the frame altogether. It is obviously necessary to move the artwork down (South) at this point and this can only be done by moving the entire set-up as it stands. To accomplish this, two rails (or tubes) are built into the base (or the shooting table) and a platform runs along them on ball-bearings; a worm screw can be used to drive the platform in the North-South direction. The animation table with its pegbars and rotation unit is then placed on this platform. Now we have an assembly which is capable of making almost any compound move — in fact we have a basic animation *compound*.

Diagonal pans can now be made by a compound move of the pegbar in the East-West direction and the North-South move of the entire assembly. There is indeed very little that cannot be done with this type of compound.

Leaving out the rotation

As the diagonal pans can be achieved with the use of a pegbar and compound move, you don't need the rotation for them. It could be left out of the construction if it proves difficult — and if you are not going to need rotating shots. The animation table top with its pegbars is mounted directly onto the North-South compound move.

Now this whole set-up can be placed on another set of rails (or tubes) running at right angles to give an East-West movement of the entire compound. The main advantage of this is that the artwork can be moved in any desired direction by means of the two compounds leaving the pegbars to work quite independently.

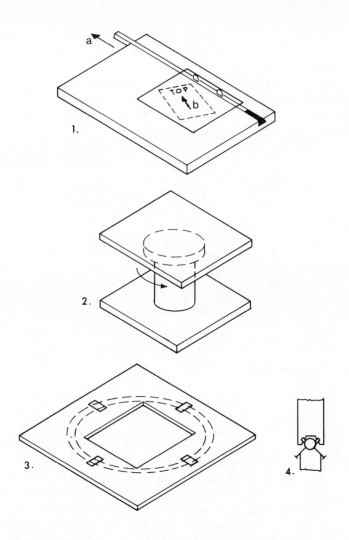

1, When diagonal pans are made with a pegbar it is necessary to mount the artwork in line to the vertical and horizontal of the camera; (a) direction of pan (b) vertical position of the artwork. 2, Rotating the table top is not too difficult where there is no backlight consideration. 3, Backlight area must be left clear. 4, A track should have bearings for ease of rotation.

For example, a car is moving from right to left across the frame on the bottom set of pegs while the background is panned much faster in the opposite direction on the top peg-bar; at a certain point we want to move ahead of the car and slightly up to reveal a large welcome sign on the bridge ahead. This you can do with the compound movement, while the animation of the car and the background continue without interruption.

Floating pegbar

A further possible addition is a pegbar with one set of register pins only which is supported independently of all compound moves. It is attached to the base, or the column supporting the camera and lies in a fixed position to the surface of the animation table. Its primary use is to keep a piece of artwork in a fixed position in relation to the camera while all the rest of the artwork is panned in various directions by compound and travelling peg-bar moves.

Pantograph table

Movements in a straight line, even at different speeds, are comparatively easy to work out with wheels and counters. Once you start to combine moves in different directions, and possibly rotations as well, it becomes much harder to visualise the results. If you are moving the whole animation table (on the compound movements rather than making peg-bar moves) you can follow the moves with a pointer. For this you use a pantograph table.

This is a small table attached to the base for external reference to compound moves. A pointer is attached to the animation table. As the compound moves this pointer moves over the pantograph table. On the table, you can mark the start and end of various pans as well as the central (master) position of the compound. It is also indispensable where the pan is required to follow a curved path such as the figure of eight. You plot the moves on a shot key, and

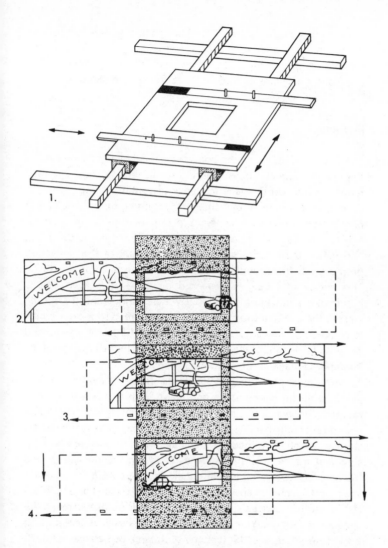

1, The compound. Diagonal moves can be made by using the pegbar and north-south movement of the complete table. Giving the table an east-west movement frees the pegbars for other uses. 2, 3, Cel of car and background are panned separately to portray movement. 4, Compound movement pans south while peg pans continue.

mark each frame position. Then you place the shot key *upside-down* on the pantograph table relative to the position of the artwork on the shooting table. Now, you move the table so that the pointer indicates each successive frame, and shoot it.

Fairings

The use of counters on the compound movements as well as on the moving pegbar makes it easier to calculate fairings. The total length of the pan in space (distance in centimetres or inches) is divided by the number of frames (representing the total length of pan in time) to obtain a constant increment. This constant increment is represented as a unit of measure, i.e. 1.5 in or 0.75 cm. The fairing then means increasing the amount of the movement progressively from nought to the constant increment or vice-versa. The choice of fairing is governed by the kind of pan that is required. A pan can be continuously increasing in speed from the start to the end of a shot; this can be represented by a curve which is continually climbing. On the other hand the fairing can spread over the full length of the shot in such a way that as the end of the fairing-in is reached – the slow-out begins.

However most pans move at constant increments for most of their length; and the fairing up to and down from this constant increment can generally be classified as: fast, medium and slow. A fast fairing takes only a few frames, and just manages to overcome the shudder which an immediate move at constant speed produces. A slow fairing takes a lot more frames to accomplish the change and the resultant curve is a lot smoother. For example, if the constant speed is 10, you can speed up: 2, 4, 6, 8 – 10 (constant); this is a fast speed up because it has taken only four frames to reach the constant increment. You can make it twice as slow by fairing: 1, 2, 3, 4, 5, 6, 7, 8, 9 – 10 (constant). Taking two frames at each fairing increment – 1, 1, 2, 2, 3, 3, 4, 4, 5, 5, etc. slows it down even further.

The choice of the precise number of frames to be taken up by the fairing is determined also by the actual value of the constant incre-

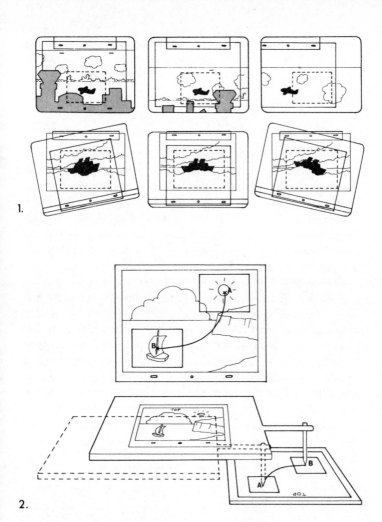

1, Floating pegbar. A floating pegbar allows the cel to be held in position independently of the table movement. In the above example the airport background is panned away from the aeroplane cel.

2, pantograph table. The shot key is placed down on the pantograph table relative to the artwork.

ment. For example, with a constant rate of 32 units, you may go 2, 4, 8, 16, 32, for a very fast start – or you may go up 1, 2, 4, 6, 8, 10, 13, 16, 19, 23, 27, 32 for a slower fairing in.

Fairing extends the pan in time

The length of a pan is 10 inches (measured from the centre of the starting field-size to the centre of the finishing one) and the number of frames is 40 (length of pan in time) then the constant increment will be $10:40 = 0.25$ inches (2.5 counter units). Using a five frame speed-up: $\frac{1}{2}$, 1, $1\frac{1}{2}$, 2, $2\frac{1}{2}$ (constant) we will have travelled a total of 0.5 in over 4 frames; at constant increment we would have travelled 1 in over 4 frames; this discrepancy of 0.5 inch is equal to 2 frames at constant increment and will therefore result in the total pan taking 42 frames to complete (if there is no slowing out). If the slow out is also done at the same rate two more frames will be added to the overall length of the pan making it 44 frames. In most cases this is not too important and it is sufficient to be aware that the extension to the pan is inevitable in this way so that you are not surprised when the things do not add up at the end of the pan. However, very long, gradual fairings can add quite a substantial number of frames to the total length of the pan.

FAIRING-IN MOVES TYPICAL EXAMPLES

Constant speed (units)	Speed-up length (frames)	Distance per frame	Constant speed equivalent
$2\frac{1}{2}$	5	$\frac{1}{2}$ 1 $1\frac{1}{2}$ 2 $2\frac{1}{2}$	2
$2\frac{1}{2}$	7	$\frac{1}{4}$ $\frac{1}{2}$ 1 $1\frac{1}{2}$ 2 $2\frac{1}{4}$ $2\frac{1}{2}$	3
5	5	1 2 3 4 5	3
10	5	2 4 6 8 10	2
10	7	1 2 4 6 8 9 10	3
15	5	$2\frac{1}{2}$ 5 $7\frac{1}{2}$ 10 $12\frac{1}{2}$ 15	$1\frac{1}{2}$
15	15	1 2 3 4 5 6 7 8 9 10 11 12 13 14 15	7

Adjusting field sizes

If the length of the pan in time (i.e. No. of frames) is very critical then the length of the pan (i.e. distance from centre to centre of the two extreme field sizes) can be altered. This is done most efficiently by adjusting the field size. You can shorten the pan with slightly larger field sizes (provided you are not already working on the maximum size). Adjust the framing so that the outer vertical edges of frame still run along the same line as before; because of the increase in the field size, the centres of the two field sizes are now nearer to each other. The total distance has been shortened. If the fairing produces 4 extra frames at a constant of 0.25 in then an overall shortening of the pan should be exactly 1 in.

The adjustment of the field size in the opposite direction, i.e. reduction in the field sizes, produces an extension of the total distance between the two field sizes. This can prove useful when the original distance is difficult to divide into a manageable unit.

Fairing and diagonal pans

When a diagonal pan is made with the aid of a moving pegbar only (as described earlier) the fairing is naturally done in the same way as for a horizontal pan. However the need for special pegging when the animation table is twisted out, combined with a frequent necessity to have more than one pan within the same shot, means that this type of diagonal panning is rather inadequate.

If a North-South movement of the compound is available, it is very often easier to make diagonal pans by moving the pegbar in the East-West plane and the compound in the North-South one. Where a compound movement in both directions can be used, the diagonal pan can be made in any direction with the compound. Then the pegbar is left free to be used for East-West panning of the artwork within the picture area.

The direction of the pan governs whether the increments are added or subtracted on both pans – or one may be adding while the other is subtracting. This may be somewhat disconcerting and it is advisable to stick down a piece of tape next to the control wheel or on the wheel itself; an arrow drawn on the tape serves as a reminder of the direction in which the wheel should be turned. Naturally, a diagonal pan made in this way must be speeded up and slowed out as any other pan. As there are two moves to be made instead of only one, this can present a few problems. A diagonal pan at 45° to the horizontal of the picture frame is relatively easy because both East-West and North-South moves are identical in length. The constant increments are the same for both of these moves and therefore fairings calculated for one move apply to the other. It is not too difficult to calculate the fairings on diagonal pans if there is a convenient ratio between the two moves. As we have just noted a 45° diagonal pan requires both East-West and North-South to move an equal amount in a particular direction — the result is a 1:1 ratio between the two moves. Any other angle requires a longer pan to be made by one of the compound movements than by the other. If this happens to be in the ratio of 2:1 then the increments and fairing can still be worked out for one of the moves only and then doubled or halved as the case may be.

A little bit of manipulation of the field sizes can always produce a convenient ratio between the two movements. It is most important to make these two moves correlate with each other exactly in a fixed ratio if the pan is to follow a straight line; without dipping during the fairing.

Zooms and pans

Very often a pan from one position to the next may also require a change in the field size between the two. The result is that the camera is zooming at the same time as the artwork is being moved from one position to the next. Naturally both of these moves have to be correlated in some way although this is not as critical in this case as in the case of the diagonal pans. After all these are two independent moves which can accept considerable variation; whereas the diagonal pan is a single movement visually although it

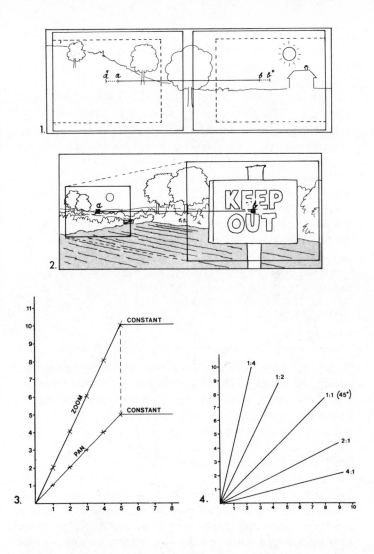

1, An adjustment in the field size can extend or shorten the pan. 2, Zoom and pan. 3, Zoom and pan fairing-in graph. 4, A workable ratio between the east-west and north-south movements should be a major consideration when planning diagonal pans.

is obtained by making a double move on the animation table. The constant increments of the zoom and the pan are unlikely to be the same especially as they are calculated in different units of measure. But it is important to try and make the zoom and pan start and end together — unless you want a specific effect. It is also quite useful to make the fairings of equal length in number of frames (or as close as possible) because of the ease of operation which results from this; greater concentration is required when shooting the fairings than when all moves are made at their respective constant increments.

Zooms and pans can not only be made to follow completely different fairings but they can follow entirely different curves. For example, the pan may be at a constant speed throughout its length apart from speed up and slow outs at the start and finish while the zoom also starts with a speed up but it has two constant rates; i.e. it moves slower at first and then accelerates and continues to move at a faster rate.

Strobing

In our early example of a six-sided pencil rolling along the table we noticed the effects of strobing when the amount of movement made per frame is too great. Turning the pencil 5/6 of its circumference (five facets) for each frame of picture results in the pencil appearing to rotate in the opposite direction to that in which it is seen to be moving. Most cinemagoers are familiar with this effect on the spokes of carriage wheels.

You can get the same effect when you pan. It is usually easier to cope with in live action filming than in animation. A very fast camera move produces blurred images. This is better than seeing a number of clear distinct images. If you move animation artwork a great amount each frame, the strobing is inevitable just because each frame is a sharp clear picture individually photographed.

It is not always possible to predict with absolute certainty at what point a certain move will begin to strobe because there are so many different factors determining this. But as far as panning is concerned it is possible to calculate at which point strobing is likely to become a real danger. If you divide 100 by the field size (f, in inches) the number which you obtain this way will be the number of frames per inch of the pan (S, the speed) beyond which the strobing becomes a risk.

i.e. $S = \dfrac{100}{f \text{ (D) in inches}}$

Other factors contributing to the appearance of strobing are high contrast subjects, thin lines and repetitive features.

Strobing appears also within the animated artwork itself when extremely large movements are made; as a general rule of thumb the subject should not move more than half its width (judged along the line of travel) per frame. So if an arm is to move down from a raised position each successive drawing of the line should not be farther from the preceding one than half the thickness of the arm. Inevitably this means that thicker shapes can be made to move faster than thinner ones without the risk of strobing. This is particularly useful to remember in connection with lettering – thinner letters begin to strobe sooner than thicker ones.

However, the speed dictated by these considerations of strobing can be completely wrong for the desired effect to be achieved. Suppose a hand moves from a raised position and lands its fist on the desk. A move of this kind must be made in fewer frames than the strobing considerations suggest if the idea of "slamming the fist on the table in anger" is to be got across to the viewer. This is where the dry-brush technique comes to the rescue; the arm is painted on the number of cells dictated by the action but instead of it being clearly outlined as before it is now smeared. The result is an impression of a very fast movement of the arm but without the distracting effects of strobing.

Whip pans

Strobing can be ignored completely or even used deliberately in certain cases, such as whip (swish) pans. These are pans that whip across from one view to the next and have a great dramatic shoc.. value. Even when large distances between field sizes are involved whip pans should not be longer than 3 to 8 frames. Fairing can be ignored for this type of effect pan.

The whip pan can be used not only to connect a series of images from the same piece of artwork in a dramatic succession but it can be used as a link between entirely different pieces of artwork. The pictures should always be framed in such a way that there is a fair amount of room for the pan in the desired direction. Half way through the whip pan, the artwork is changed and the movement continues at the same rate.

When it is not possible to use the same field size for the two scenes which are to be linked by a whip pan, then it is important to find a convenient ratio between their field sizes so that the speed of pan can be adjusted accordingly. This way the apparent difference in sizes of the artwork will not be noticeable.

Zooming and strobing

Strobing is only a serious danger to zooming shots when it also involves a pan. It should be remembered that the strobing is more likely to occur at the smaller field-sizes and the precautionary calculations should be done with the smaller field sizes of the zoom regardless of whether it is a zoom-in or out, and ignoring the wider field size.

Crash zooms

Like the whip pans these can be very effective aids in adding drama to a scene. They work even at two or three frames, with the best results at about four frames. Slower speeds beyond six frames produce results more like fast zooms than real crashing effects. The best crash-zooms are those where the centres of the two field sizes are close together. The crash zoom can work well on the zoom out as well as the zoom in. The framing of the smaller

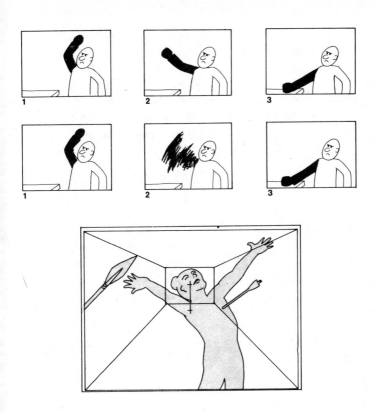

Fast movement. Dry-brush technique is used to give a blured image to the in-between cels when the speed of the action is likely to make it strobe.

Crash zooms have great impact, especially when the centres of the two field sizes are close.

field size is of great importance because this is the point to which the attention of the audience is being directed. It should be within the area of the larger field, so that the object of importance is there to be seen in the larger context either before the crash zoom or after it. It is also advisable to have static hold at the start or the end of the crash zoom (if not both) for the same reason.

Camera Movements with Solid Objects

The zoom lens

The use of the zoom lens in the animation of solid objects is much the same as in the shooting of flat artwork animation. It should always be focused at the extreme narrow angle setting to ensure that it holds focus over its full range (even when the full range of the zoom is not actually used). Just as with flat artwork, you may want your own calibration scale and pointer. However, unlike flat artwork shooting, the effect of a zoom is not identical with that of a track.

Difference between tracking and zooming

When the camera tracks-in from a position farther away from flat artwork to a position nearer to it the result on projection is a zoom in. There is no real difference between this zoom and one covering the same range done using a zoom lens. When it comes to shooting three dimensional objects the difference between the zoom and track become apparent. When tracking we are in effect using a lens of a fixed focal length (even if it is a zoom lens at a fixed setting) and the angle of view remains constant. Because of this, the perspective changes with the distance from the object per partial, relative distances between objects appear more realistic. The zoom lens changes its focal length (within a specified range); this means that the angle of view changes with the variation in the focal length during the zoom.

At the short focal length end the zoom has all the characteristics of a fixed lens of short focal length; convergence and an increased feeling of distance in depth between objects and the background. On the other hand the long focal length end has the characteristics of a fixed focal length telephoto lens; foreshortening of the distance between objects and background (compression) and a sharp decrease in the depth of field (see page 107).

The compression of the scene can destroy the feeling of solidarity; in addition, when cutting to another angle of view which is shot with focal length nearer to standard, a discrepancy between apparent distances between objects may become noticeable. This is a distraction which can ruin the continuity of the scene.

Tracking

A horizontal set-up similar to the one used sometimes for shooting flat animation is suitable for tracking shots. Tracking in a straight line produces much the same effect as zooming (particularly in flat artwork animation). In fact, a really smooth, steady track can have distinct advantages over a zoom lens when it comes to very slow zooms (or tracks). You can divide the whole length of the track into increments. In addition the camera may be driven along the track by a worm-screw drive, a control wheel and a counter indicating the number of revolutions can be used to give an even more accurate and finer division of the total move. A lathe bed is an ideal tracking device but a solid camera platform on ball-bearing wheels and running on metal rails can be just as good.

An electric motor can be coupled to the drive shaft to facilitate speedy returns to start position and rough test runs; in some cases it can also be used to move the camera on during the shooting. This is not suitable when very small increments are involved – this is better done manually. A DC motor is more suitable for use when it can be speeded up and slowed down with a simple variable resistor. On those occasions when continuous shooting can be used instead of stop-motion (i.e. when there is no animation to be done in front of the camera in-between frames) then the entire shot can be "motorised".

It is important that there are no excessive vibrations from the drive motor. Stand a glass of water on the camera and watch it during a test run. There should hardly be a ripple. In addition it is advisable always to shoot at slower camera speeds than the one representing real time — i.e. projection speed. This way you have a better chance of making the shot last a predetermined period. It also gives you more operating time which makes it easier to speed up, and slow out to a stop at a predetermined point. Test runs can be made against a stop-watch to determine the maximum speed required for covering the distance of track.

Of course, you could track with flat artwork. But, as we explained, it is easier to work on a vertical set-up and, in this case, zooming and tracking produce exactly the same effect.

Zooming and tracking

The effective range of the zoom lens can be increased if it is combined with a track. However the changeover from tracking to zooming is very likely to be noticeable and should be covered up by some deliberate changes in the action in front of the camera. Two zooms whose speeds vary deliberately and are related to the action can be done this way. A zoom in two parts can also be done as a combination of a zoom and track — first part of the zoom done on the track and the second with the zoom lens.

The zoom lens can be operated simultaneously while tracking to give a really smooth and effective extension of the zoom — provided the focus is also altered progressively through the shot.

Follow focus

The main advantage of the use of a zoom lens is that the focus remains fixed on the same plane during the full range of the zoom. Tracking, however, requires a continuous alteration in focus as the camera approaches the object being photographed. This operation is known as following the focus. Check and mark key positions on the focus ring — start and end of track and a couple in between. Divide the distances by the number of frames (length of the shot in time); this can be done on a separate piece of tape which is then attached to the focus ring. If the increments are too small per frame then the focus ring can be operated on every two or three frames. Take care, though, large jumps in the follow focus can be very distracting – even when there is no noticeable change in sharpness; this is because the manipulation of focus also alters the image size. You can make an extension pointer and a correspondingly bigger scale to fit round the lens.

Auto follow focus

If you intend to make extensive use of tracks, it is worth thinking in terms of an automatic follow focus system. This eases the shooting operation considerably. This is particularly important for those whose cameras are not fitted with a zoom or the range of their zoom lens is not very great. There are two ways to make a follow-focus system.

One is to place a long metal strip along the camera track. Cut this to shape by taking focus checks at a number of points along the track. A roller runs along the cam thus cut. This raises a rack and pinion mechanism against a spring to follow the cam shape. The pinion is fitted to turn the focus ring on the lens.

The second method employs a circular cam, which pushes a lever in and out to rotate a focus ring. The cam itself is rotated (through gears) by means of a rack and pinion – the rack lying along the full length of the track. This method allows for the use of more than one lens on those cameras with interchangeable lens facility. A separate cam has to be cut for each lens, but they are much easier to change than full-length cams.

If you want to make an auto-focus system for a zoom lens, cut the cam for its long focal length setting.

A tracking set up does not always have to be used with the camera facing forward. It can be positioned at various angles to the track and these positions can also be varied during the shooting.

Panning

You may want to pan the camera when animating solid objects. For this, ideally, the camera should be fixed to a good, sturdy

1, General view of scene. 2, Zoom in on character. 3, Tracking in at fixed focal length.

tripod head which is in turn attached to the camera tracking system. To pan, you simply rotate the camera on the tripod head. A tape placed around the base of the tripod head can be used to indicate the start and end positions. You can take off the tape to mark necessary increments (including fairings); then put it back in position for shooting. If the tripod head is small in circumference, an extension arm can be used to give bigger and clearer increments. An old geared head of the type used in professional film making is more suitable than a normal friction tripod head because the panning wheel is a ready made control which can be divided to give accurate increments. If you want, you can attach mechanical counters to it. However, a simple geared drive system is not beyond the capacity of an enthusiast.

Tilting

Tilting the camera up and down can be done in much the same way as panning left to right. For most tripods you need a semicircular extension fitted to the plate on which the camera is resting. You can paint a permanent scale on it, indicating the angle of tilt in degrees. This, combined with a pointer attached to the base serves to indicate the increment for each move. If the scale plate is deliberately off-set, a tape can be placed along its bottom side which can be used for dividing the distance or the amount of tilt much more easily (including fairing). It is important that the pointer is set at the centre of the off-set scale when the camera is horizontal. That way, the full range of the tilt, both up and down, can be accommodated.

A geared drive, as in the case of panning, makes the shooting a lot easier – particularly as a normal tilt has to be locked off after every move to stop if from "creeping", under the weight of the camera.

Some problems

Shooting solid object animation is a kind of stylised representation of real life in miniature. By panning, tilting and tracking through

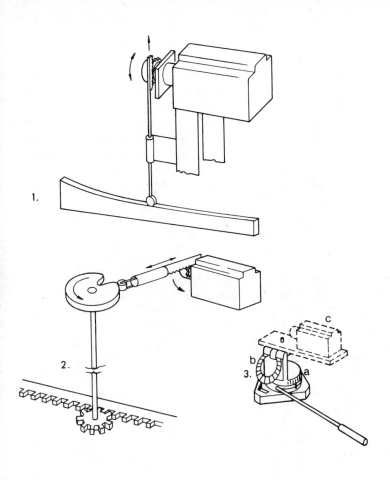

Automatic follow focus. 1, A focusing cam runs the full length of the track. 2, A spring-loaded lever is operated through a gearbox by a circular follow focus cam.

3, Adding to a pan-and-tilt head. Panning scale and pointer (a); tilting scale and pointer (b); extension plate and camera position with the lens at "nodal point" (c).

these miniatures, you can create a feeling of a real scene — more so than with flat artwork animation. The camera movements imitate the movements of a live camera in a real live situation and therefore they are expected to give the same sort of results in miniature.

Unfortunately this is not always easy to achieve because of the sheer physical size of the camera — even on 8 mm one. This is best illustrated if we compare a panning shot of a live action scene with one of the same scene in miniature. During the live action (real) pan of 180° the front of the camera lens travels a distance roughly equal to the distance the eyes of the viewer would travel if he were standing in the same place and looking at the same scene. The camera lens is situated at the same distance from the centre of rotation even when a miniature of the scene may be on a scale of 100:1. The camera lens travels the *same* distance for the 180° pan. A pan made in this way will not be much like the pan over the real scene however accurate a reproduction the miniature set may be. The miniature pan would look as if the camera were swung around on the end of a pole. A comparable effect would be achieved with the live scene by placing the camera lens (and the camera) farther away from the centre of rotation by 100× the normal distance. The same apparent movement applies to tilting shots. They make the results look like the results of full-size crane shots.

Nodal point

The pivoting point of a conventional tripod runs vertically through the centre of the tripod. The only way you get realistic panning and tilting with miniatures is to shorten the distance from the front of the lens to the pivoting centre by an amount equivalent to the reduction in the scale of the miniature. For all practical purposes, the camera can be moved back to a point where the front of the lens (actually the front nodal point) is approximately at the pivoting centre.

In practice, it is extremely difficult to modify your tripod mount to make the centre of *tilt* coincide with the lens. It is virtually always somewhat lower. When the front element of the lens coincides with the centre of pivoting, panning and tilting have the effect of an eye moving in its socket — scanning the scene without the movement of the head. With a conventional tripod you can attach a metal plate to the camera-mounting screw. Cut another hole in the plate at the appropriate distance. Fix the camera with the help of a spare screw. You may need a certain amount of counterbalancing. This depends on the length of the lens, and therefore how far back the camera needs to be moved; and on the weight of the camera itself. A sturdy, heavy duty tripod can overcome these problems with most 8 mm cameras.

Dollying

The tracks along which the camera platform runs do not necessarily have to be straight. Semicircular tracks can be made to take the camera around a puppet as well as nearer to it. These tracks are best made in sections and although they are all laid for the test run they should be detachable so they do not appear in the picture. As the camera platform approaches the end of one section the new section is joined on. Large gauge model railway tracks may be suitable to support a light camera.

Craning

An ordinary tripod can be used to support the camera if the miniature set is made on a rostrum at a convenient working level. In addition the rostrum itself can be made on the lines of a revolving stage. This is useful for changing the angles where only a limited space is available but it can present problems with the lights unless they also move with the set. Some of the tripods have a facility for varying the height which can be used for craning shots: the camera changing height during the shot. This can be a useful move particularly for those who are restricted to using full size tripods.

Composite moves

Very often, several camera moves need to be made simultaneously for the same shot. The procedure for this is to find the start and end position for each movement, divide their respective distances by the number of frames the move is expected to take and make up a separate scale for each movement involved.

During the shooting it is very important to follow a predetermined routine or cycle. This reduces the chance of making some moves twice, or missing out others completely. Remember that there are movements of figures to be made also. You may find it better if some part of the operation can be delegated to an understanding helper. Don't mix up your jobs, though.

After that astounding shot when you've got everything on the go, slow down and settle into some ordinary, simple shots where the camera is absolutely static. By now your viewer will be more interested in the content rather than the trickery. When you do zoom, or make any other camera movement, make sure first that it is really necessary. Then be sure that your chosen way is most practical in terms of time and effort required. Do ambitious shots only when they're justified by the storyline.

Fairing the moves

Virtually all camera moves should be speeded up at the start and slowed out at the end. This again should correspond to the way in which the camera would be operated during continuous live action shooting. A pan or a track never starts with a sudden jerk – moves on at a constant rate and then stops just as suddenly. Yet this is precisely what would happen if the total distance of any of the camera moves was divided into equal increments and shot single frame. See the previous chapter for details of fairing curves and methods of working out the fairings. They apply just as much for three dimensional objects as for flat artwork.

Strobing

Strobing again is something that has been dealt with more fully in an earlier chapter. It should be borne in mind that strobing is a common headache to all aspects of cinematography and you need to pay a lot of attention to avoiding its occurrence. The animation of three dimensional objects is particularly prone to this because the camera movements here are essentially replicas of camera movements during continuous shooting. Unlike the case of continuous shooting where the move can be made too fast so that the image is smeared, in stop frame shooting each frame is as good and sharp as the preceding one regardless of the increase in the increment of the move. Of course, you can't use a dry-brush technique with solid things. The only way with this type of work is to make the movements at speeds below the suspected strobing point. This point, of course, varies with the subject matter and can be worked out in much the same way as in the case of the shooting of flat artwork animation. (See page 78.)

As a general rule: when in doubt, use a slightly wider angle, because the smaller the area being photographed (narrow lens angle) the faster the apparent speed of the movement. In those circumstances where there is no animation to be done of the objects in front of the camera during a fast pan it may be possible to shoot continuously and achieve a blurring effect. Slower camera speeds are preferred for this as they mean (in most cases) longer exposure times resulting in greater chance of the camera actually moving during the exposure of each frame.

The Camera

The camera is the single most important item of equipment you need for shooting animation. Consequently, you should pay a great deal of attention in choosing the most suitable camera for this purpose. Some makes of 8 mm cameras have almost all the facilities normally found on the professional 16 mm and 35 mm cameras, specially designed for animation. True, they are in the upper price range, but they are still far less expensive than their professional counterparts. For most purposes in animation as far as the cameras are concerned, 8 mm facilities are basically just as good as those of other guages.

Single frame (stop motion) facility

A single frame facility is, of course, the pre-requisite for all animation shooting. It means that a series of individual pictures (Frames) can be exposed in succession and at whatever interval of time may be needed between each exposure. The exposure time should be identical for every frame. That ensures that when the completed shot (consisting of a series of these separately exposed pictures) is projected, it should appear perfectly even throughout its length. The best way of testing this is to do a static shot of some inanimate object at normal continuous run, and then do the same shot again as a series of single frames. On projection, the two shots should look exactly the same. Any variation in the exposure time per frame shows up as a flickering image (like the early movies). Such a test also shows you whether the exposure time when shooting single frame is the same as when shooting at a specific camera speed setting for continuous operation. This should not be taken for granted, because on most cameras continuous shooting exposure time varies with the camera speed but the single frames exposure is fixed. You need to establish the relationship, to see if it is possible to use occasional bursts of continuous shooting during the holds in animation.

The steady test

This is another important test to be done with a new camera. It will help you to establish just how good the registration of your camera movement is. It should certainly be done with older cameras where there is a risk that the camera mechanism may have suffered from wear and tear. The test consists of shooting single frame exposure on evenly lit black card with a series of vertical and horizontal white lines painted on it. On projection, the projection aperture is adjusted so that the line between frames is visible on the screen. Any unsteadiness will be indicated by a movement of the white lines above the frame line in relation to those below the frame line. If there is more than the slightest quiver, you cannot expect to shoot really good animation.

An additional test is to expose the same card twice on the same piece of film. For the second exposure, move the card diagonally by about half the distance between the white lines on it. On normal projection any unsteadiness will show up as a shift between the two exposures of the grid. Of course, this test cannot be done without a windback facility (see page 111).

Remote control

Very often, the animator is at some distance from the camera manipulating the puppets or changing the artwork. Reaching out for the single frame release button or walking over to the camera can be rather a waste of energy. Remote control operation of the camera is virtually essential for any serious work. Basically there are two types: mechanical and electronic. A lot of camera makes have one or both of these facilities supplied as accessories. The electronically operated remote control is the best because of the freedom of movement this gives to the operator. The mechanical operation is normally intended for use with a cable release. A small solenoid motor can be used to operate the single frame release button directly on the camera or through a cable release. A 12 V battery, a length of cable and a contact button are all that is required to give the operator complete freedom to move as far away from the camera as he likes.

Counters

All cameras have some means of indicating the amount of film used, but for animation purposes a footage counter is not sufficient. Because animation is done in frames it is important to have an accurate frame counter which gives clear and precise counts. Ideally, this frame counter should also be resettable so that each new shot can be started at zero. Unfortunately the frame counters on most cameras fall short of the ideal on many counts. They are usually too small and placed in such inaccessible places that it is virtually impossible to keep referring to them constantly during the shooting as is really necessary for animation work.

Ideally, the counter should be at the operator's fingertips and close to the single frame release button. For this, it must be remotely operated.

Ordinary cameras cannot be fitted with such a counter. So, the only way to do it is to use a separate electronic counter wired up to the remote control release button. Every time you press the button an electronic impulse is sent to the counter, which then registers one frame. You use the same type of counters we described earlier for other functions so it is easy to incorporate them into a remote control panel. The frame counter is the animator's only indication of "real time" and should be referred to continually. If the camera counter is good enough, it should be used as a back up to double check the electronic counter. Additionally, as the electronic counter can be reset at zero at any point during the animation, the camera counter can serve a useful purpose in indicating a cumulative total.

Cell animation. A zoom in and superimposed flash can be shot with just one piece of artwork.

Movements within the frame demand carefully registered cels of the moving part.

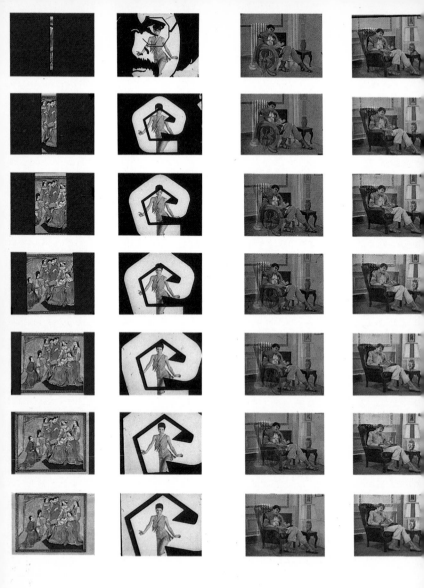

Masking off parts of the scene – in this case flat artwork – can produce wipes, or more complicated reveals.

By rotoscoping from a live action scene, you can produce a matching piece of flat copy. Mix from one to the other to produce a transformation.

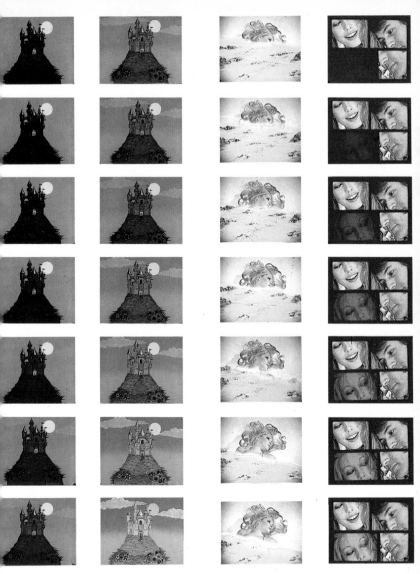

Another mix transformation. This time with two pieces of carefully matched artwork.

A wipe following the natural action of a wave can mix one scene into the next.

By introducing a split screen, you can add considerably to the impact of a piece of flat artwork.

You can superimpose a flash over live artwork, here coinciding with a focus pull.

White titles, too, can be superimposed. Zooming and fading adds interest.

With suitable mattes, you can zoom out, then reveal a piece of artwork sector by sector.

Perhaps the simplest form of animation is silhouetted cut-outs. Changing or moving pieces between single frames produces the movement.

With split screen, you can mix in a single piece of artwork in sections.

Slit-scan effects can be controlled by altering the slit shape. Cutting it to match a subject, such as the fountain produces a radiating effect. In this sequence, it has mixed into a "straight" slit-scan.

By interrupting the length of scan, the slit can be made to move out (or in) to any position. If the top lit artwork is unlit, the slit produces a silhouette effect.

Slit-scan effects can be used for static patterns too.

Page 104: Using a Zoptic back projection screen, you can combine a normally-lit puppet with a back-ground in a single shot. The bottom picture shows a simple set-up.

Viewfinder

The majority of 8 mm cameras are equipped with reflex viewfinders which facilitate direct through-the-lens viewing. Although
the shooting of flat artwork animation can be done without a reflex
viewfinder, a separate viewfinder is a distinct disadvantage for
shooting puppet and other three dimensional animation. This is
mainly because you are working at such relatively close range that
it is difficult to compensate successfully for the parallax.

The viewfinder is used in animation only for lining up and not
during actual single frame shooting. It is because of this that a
camera with a non-reflex viewfinder can be used quite successfully
on a set-up for flat artwork animation. This is done with the aid of
rotoscoping.

Rotoscoping for non-reflex cameras

When the film cartridge is removed, it is possible to place a small
mirror behind the aperture at 45° to the film plane. Then put a
piece of clear film in the camera aperture. Direct a light via a mirror
at this piece of film in the aperture. Open the shutter and this turns
the camera into a projector. The film is projected by the camera
lens onto the shooting table below. With the lens iris fully open
and a white card on the shooting table a small light source is sufficient to give an image. If the camera is equipped with a zoom
lens then you can mark up the various field sizes alongside the
focal length scale. (Alternatively you can prepare a chart giving the
relative image sizes at the various focal lengths). Indicate the centre on the shooting table, or if there is a moving compound, then
set it at the central position. You can also indicate this with a
reference to the pantograph table, which (if there is one) is always
fixed.

If the camera is not equipped with a zoom lens, then the various
field sizes are indicated along the column along which the camera
support is moved. (The pantograph reference for the compound
remains the same in both cases). If the camera mount is moved

along the support column by a mechanical drive (which also has a counter attached to it) — then it is possible to make a chart giving the counter reading for the various field sizes. Once you have done all this, it is possible to shoot with a non-reflex camera just as well as with a reflex one.

Rotoscoping for reflex cameras

Rotoscoping through the camera gate requires the shutter to be in the open position; this is not always possible with some makes of camera. However rotoscoping through the viewfinder can be done with any reflex viewfinder. You may want to do that to check the accuracy of the viewfinder by comparing the two images. However its most valuable use is to facilitate the projection of a frame of picture for the correct line up of titles (see camera effects page 158). The reflex viewfinder is ideal for rotoscoping through while the film is still in the camera (unlike rotoscoping through the aperture of a camera gate). A set up designed for shooting flat artwork animation should include a small rotoscope lamp permanently fixed to the camera support; so that it can easily be swung into position over the eyepiece. This makes for very quick and accurate lining up as it leaves the animator free to move the artwork on the animation compound to find the correct framing. The viewfinder is needed only in its normal way for checking focus. Be careful though, you can damage the eyepiece lenses if the light is so powerful as to overheat them.

Camera lenses

The lenses on the majority of 8 mm cameras are permanently fixed to the camera body. However, a few cameras have the facility to interchange their lenses. If, so, you can fit lenses of various focal lengths, including some normally used on still cameras (with appropriate adaptors). Prime lenses (fixed focal length lenses) generally produce higher image quality than that of equivalent quality zoom lenses. The interchangeable lens system allows greater flexibility in use not only of prime lenses but of zoom lenses also. So, you can choose a zoom lens of just the focal length range you want.

Macro focusing

Extreme close-ups can be done with normal prime lenses using a supplementary close-up lens (often called a dioptre). Close-up lenses are lens elements of various magnification which are placed in front of the lens to enable it to focus closer. The lens is normally set at infinity and the camera moved nearer or farther away from the object to get it in sharp focus.

Another method is to fit extension tubes between the camera body and the lens. This, of course, can only be used with those cameras which have the interchangeable lens facility.

Some lenses are constructed with a built-in "macro-focusing" ability, and need no additional attachments. The main advantage of these lenses is that the focus can be moved from an object in extreme close up to another one at a distance where a normal prime lens would be able to focus – during the same shot; this of course cannot be done with a normal prime lens using close up attachments.

Zoom lenses

The zoom lens is a lens with the facility for varying the focal length within a certain predetermined range. The quality of these lenses is judged by their resolving power, their ability to keep good focus throughout their full range of focal lengths and the extent of that range. For animation purposes a ratio of 4:1 between the widest and the narrowest angles is barely adequate; anything less is not really much use. This is one field where the ratios of 10:1 and more offer greater scope.

Although their overall ratio may be the same, zoom lenses vary in focal lengths. Whether long focus or wide angle is more important depends on your animation. An extremely wide angle can be a problem when shooting flat artwork animation whereas it is a distinct advantage in the shooting of models. Always bear in mind that zoom lenses can and should be used as normal prime lenses and fight the temptation to zoom in and out on every shot. Accessory lenses for close up focusing can be used with the zoom lenses in the same way as with the prime lenses – if they are treated as prime lenses. The focus tends to disappear very rapidly if you attempt conventional zooming with the close up attachments fitted. This in itself can be a very useful effect.

A macro focusing facility is built in as a standard part in some zoom lenses. Although a useful accessory, the macro facility is more necessary in shooting of solid animation than in flat artwork animation. Check how your "macro" facility works. Some operate only on the widest angle of the zoom, which may be restrictive. In fact, if that is the case, you may find that choosing the camera with the widest angle zoom available is a real disadvantage for macro focusing.

Motorised zoom lenses

Many zoom lenses fitted to 8 mm cameras are motorised in some way. This is not a feature you normally need for animation. For that, you are better off with manual zooming. Most motorised lenses can be operated manually as well. Don't try to use one without it. A motorised zoom lens with a variable speed control can also be used at very low speed settings, but still you will find small movements difficult to do accurately.

Lens iris

The iris diaphragm controls the amount of light that reaches the film in the camera gate. It works much the same as the iris of an eye, closing down to admit less light and opening up to allow a lot more light. The amount of light that passes through the iris is indicated in terms of f stops (sometimes T stops). The widest f stop

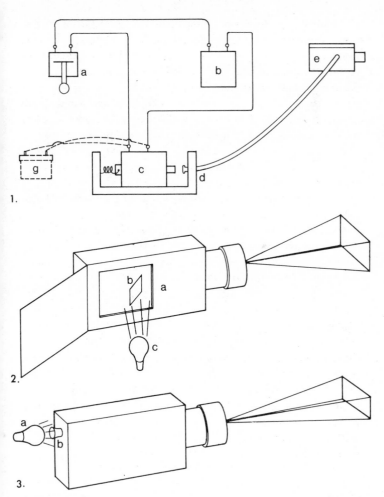

1, Electric wiring for a remote control/cable operation. (a) Contact breaker; (b) battery (12 V); (c) solenoid motor; (d) cable release; (e) camera. An electronic counter can also be incorporated (g).

2, Rotoscoping through the camera gate. (a) Camera gate; (b) mirror at 45° (or prism); (c) light source.

3, Rotoscoping through the reflex viewfinder. (a) Light source; (b) eyepiece (rubber removed).

is determined by the design of the lens. It is characterised by the lowest *f* number (e.g. *f*1.3, *f*1.8 etc.).

At the widest *f* stop, the light rays pass through the widest area of the lens. This produces a shallow depth of field. Also, any defects in the lens show up as a softening of resolution. When the iris is stopped down (closed down) only those light rays which pass through the central area of the lens elements are allowed to reach the film. The depth of field increases. The resolving power of the lens is at its best somwhere around the middle of its range. Naturally a lot of light is required to facilitate the use of a small *f* stop and this is not always possible.

Cameras with automatic exposure control have their lens iris operated electronically in response to the exposure meter. This is a distinct disadvantage in shooting animation and it is essential for the camera to have a manual override so that the iris setting is not subject to any undesirable changes during the shooting.

The *f* stops are indicated on the iris ring or in the viewfinder and calibrated as *f*2, 2.8; 4; 5.6; 8; 11; 16; 22. The range depends on the design of the lens. For animation, you may wish to calculate the aperture scale more precisely, in thirds or even quarter stops. Some lenses are fitted with irises that can be stopped down to an absolute closed position so that no light is allowed through at all. Fade and mix (dissolve) devices sometimes make use of this type of iris. This too can be useful in animation.

Depth of field

The range of focus in front and beyond the primary focus of the lens is referred to as depth of field. Lack of depth of field does not present any great problems in the shooting of flat artwork animation unless the artwork is on more than one level; e.g. a thick book placed over a newspaper, where both have to be sharp. Alternatively, you may want your artwork on several levels, at some distance from each other and lit separately. In this case and in the case of all solid objects it is absolutely essential to understand just how to control depth of field to give you the desired result.

As we have already seen, one of the primary factors affecting the depth of field is the iris setting: the smaller *f* stop used, the shallower the depth of field, and vice versa.

Another factor is the focal length of the lens: lenses of shorter focal lengths (wide angle) have greater depths of field than those of longer focal length (at a particular *f* stop). This means that in the case of the zoom lenses the depth of field changes with the variation of the acceptance angle of the lens. Therefore, when you use a zoom lens at a particular focal length, it has the same characteristics as a fixed focal length lens of the same focal length. As the depth changes with a zoom, you must be quite sure of the effect when shooting animation. It can be disconcerting for part of a scene to go all fuzzy as you zoom in.

Another factor affecting the depth of field is nearness to the object being photographed. The nearer the camera is to this object the shallower the depth of field becomes. This is particularly noticeable at long focal lengths and at short focus distances. This gives quite a nice effect and can be exploited deliberately. It can however, make it difficult to achieve realism when working with models.

To ensure the greatest possible depth of field may mean shifting the primary focus from the main object of interest. The ideal distance is approximately one third farther away than the distance of the nearest point which is in sharp focus. It is wisest to make a visual check — possible with some viewfinders. If the depth of field is not enough, you will have to stop down the lens until it is. Of course, you have to increase the light level correspondingly. It is worth remembering that the depth of field encompasses a greater area beyond the point of primary focus — towards infinity, than from the same point towards the camera. Although the difference between the two decreases as you focus closer.

Windback facility

It is extremely useful to be able to wind back your film. It makes it possible to shoot some of the more advanced optical effects which require the same section of the film to be run more than once through the camera gate. Mixes (dissolves), double exposures, split-screening, etc. (see Camera Effects) are all done by putting the film through more than once.

Unfortunately, very few makes of Super 8 mm cameras are equipped with this facility which is really a pre-requisite for any sophsticated optical effects. Super 8 film can be backwound only to a limited extent (up to about 100 frames) in some cameras (intended for making fades). Single-8 and Standard-8 films both allow backwinding right through the reel.

Some Single-8 cameras are made with backwinding (and reverse filming) facilities. Standard-8 cameras are no longer made. You can still find them on the used camera market. If you want to concentrate on animation, you will have to acquire a camera with backwind. So, the alternatives are to shoot Single-8 (which is identical in format to Super-8) Standard-8 or 16 mm. You can have Super-8 prints made to go with other Super-8 material.

A certain amount of this work can be done without the rewind facility but it is tedious and wasteful on film stock because it involves unloading the camera and pushing the film back by hand. This sort of operation is best done at the head of the roll (cartridge) because of the danger of fogging the preceding take. A sync mark in the form of a notch is made on one of the frames at the head of the shot; the camera is loaded so that the sync frame is a little distance away from the gate on the upper side of it. A few single frames are then taken: this serves two purposes — to make sure the camera is taking up OK and also to bring the sync frame into the gate; after the sync frame has been taken, set the counter at zero (if it is an external re-settable type). It may be set to zero automatically when you close the camera. Now you can move a specified number of frames forward (allowing enough clearance after the sync mark to avoid the fogged section) and make the first exposure. At the end of the shot unload the camera *in the dark*, and wind the film back to the head by hand.

The loading procedure for the second pass through the camera is exactly the same as the first time. The accuracy of this sort of operation is almost wholly dependent on one factor — a good frame counter.

112

There are gadgets available which can wind the Super-8 film back a specified number of frames. The cartridge is loaded into the windback box, preferably in the dark, and a counter indicates the amount the film has been moved back. It is wiser with this sort of gadget still to use a sync mark method as described earlier especially where frame accuracy is required. The windback box enables you to shoot anywhere in the roll though, and windback with reasonable certainty that the preceding shot is not going to be fogged.

16 mm cameras

There are advantages in using 16 mm film for animation. Film stock costs are a small proportion of your outlay, and you need only a simple camera for most work. There are numerous used "amateur" 16 mm cameras that provide all the facilities you need. These cost far less than a moderately sophisticated Super-8 model. Many allow you to interchange the lens. However, they are unlikely to have a zoom lens, so you need a mechanical tracking (and associated autofocus) system.

The camera shutter

The camera shutter (positioned between the lens and the camera gate) serves to stop the light reaching the film during the intermittent transportation of the film from one frame to the next. There are two types: rotary and guillotine.

A *rotary shutter* is basically a disc with one half cut off. It is driven in mechanical interlock with the camera drive mechanism so that it makes one full rotation during one frame. During the single frame operation this means that the shutter is at the closed position at the start, it rotates around to expose the picture, and stops in the closed position again. The exposure time is then determined by the length of time it takes the shutter to perform one full rotation and is in fact equal to half of the time — because the cut off section is 180°.

A number of low light (XL) cameras have open angles greater than 180°. This allows the light to reach the film for a slightly longer time (i.e. a slower shutter speed). An electromagnetic device is often incorporated so that the shutter always stops 'closed'.

Variable shutter and fades

Most rotary shutters have their cut off area fixed at around 180°–230°. However, there are some which have an extra blade which can be operated to reduce this cut off as desired. The effect of this is to reduce the exposure time although the camera speed remains constant and therefore the shutter still takes the same amount of time to complete one rotation. This reduction of exposure follows a regular pattern: at 90° the exposure has been reduced by one stop, at 45°, by one more etc. If the shutter is progressively closed down from 180° to its fully closed position and a single frame taken at each setting you achieve a perfect fade out – the picture fades to black. The same operation repeated in reverse gives a perfect fade up (or fade in) from black to a fully exposed picture. The length of the fade is determined by the number of frames it takes for the shutter to close or open fully.

Guillotine shutters

The majority of 8 mm cameras are fitted with this type of shutter. As the name suggests a guillotine shutter has a blade which cuts off the light from the film gate during the transportation of the film from frame to frame and is withdrawn for the actual exposure. Variation in the exposure time can be achieved with this type of shutter also. So, fade control can be built in – although few cameras so equipped do actually have this facility.

Dissolves (mixes)

One of the most common misconceptions of dissolves or mixes is to think of them as just a fade out and a fade in which have been overlapped. The two shots are overlapped indeed, but the exposure of the film over this overlap section remains constant even when the scenes before and after are entirely different. In fact, one of the best tests is to dissolve out and in again *over the same shot* ! If no change of any kind is noticeable throughout, then the dissolve was successful.

When a normal fade out is overlapped with a normal fade in, there is a noticeable drop in the exposure which can be most disturbing. This is due to the fact that the progressive closing down of the shutter which produces a good, fading effect follows a different curve from that of a dissolve out (which also involves closing the shutter). During a dissolve, the relative amount of exposure which is lost on every successive frame during the closing operation has to be made up on the dissolve in. That way, each frame gets its total exposure when the two are added together. It is also extremely important for the overlaps to match for this same reason – particularly when shorter dissolves are involved.

Iris fades and dissolves

Many cameras make use of a fully closing iris to obtain the gradual reduction in exposure. Although reasonably successful with fades, this system is not so good on the dissolves. It is difficult to calibrate the iris exactly enough to keept the exposure constant.

Automatic fades and dissolves

The fade and dissolve operation is often fully automated. Some of the more sophisticated cameras have a facility to vary the length of the fade or dissolve as well as the button which puts the mechanism into operation. In some cases after a dissolve out, the windback is done automatically and the camera re-set at the correct position for a dissolve in.

These facilities are fine for straight shooting, but require careful planning if you are to get perfect results with single frame shooting.

One way to achieve fades and dissolves is to use two polaroid filters in front of your lens. As you rotate one filter over the other, you reduce the light. However, the reduction is not progressive, and you would have to calibrate your filter exactly. In addition this tends to create colour distortion.

Exposure

To ensure that the film is correctly exposed, you must pay attention to all the various factors contributing to the final result. Just as important as the correct exposure is the *consistency* of exposure; particularly in 8 mm work where the chances are that the original film will not be duplicated to give more copies (which can be evened out by the laboratory during the printing stage).

Because you expose every frame separately, continually making changes between shots, you must understand exactly how all the factors affect exposure. The light reflected from the subject (or transmitted as in the case of backlit artwork) obviously forms the basis of exposure calculations. Set up your lights, and establish the "mean" exposure you need by metering from a grey card. Once you have this mean exposure, you can treat all other exposures as derivations from it. So, if you move, dim or colour your lights, you should compare the results with your mean. This mean exposure of course is determined by the sensitivity of the film emulsion exposure time (camera speed), light intensity, lens iris setting (with all its effects on the depth of field), and lastly, something you have no control over — laboratory processing. Then you can compensate by manipulating the other factors contributing to the exposure.

These additional factors are also worth bearing in mind: the magnification ratio in extreme close-ups; reflectivity of the subject matter being photographed, and light absorption by any lens filters that may be used.

It is advisable to make out a chart which sets out the best combinations of the above elements for the standard basic exposure and refer to it whenever the need arises to compute a variation for

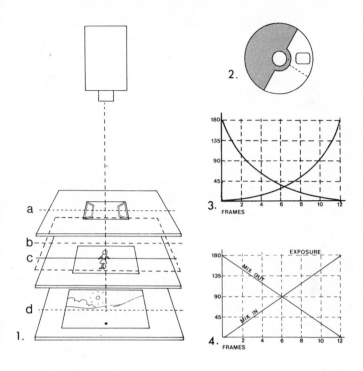

1, Multiplane artwork and hyperfocal distance. If the primary focus of the lens is at plane a, at a large *f* stop, planes c and d appear out of focus. When the focus is moved to plane c, planes a and d are out of focus. Reduce the aperture to increase the depth of field. Greatest coverage is given when focused on b – this is the hyperfocal distance in this instance.

2, An adjustable shutter angle allows simple fades. 3, The shutter angle is altered progressively from fully open to fully closed for fades. 4, For mix or dissolve work, the shutter angles on the two passes add up to the equivalent number of degrees as when the shutter is fully open.

a specific shot. When you anticipate using different film stocks, establish a "mean" exposure for each one separately, and enter it on the exposure chart.

Grey scale

The basic standard exposure should be worked out theoretically first with the help of such aids as a lightmeter; but before this is taken for granted it is wise to do a photographic test as well. The subject should ideally be black and white. representing the full range of tones from white to black. Commercial studios use a ready-made grey scale just for this purpose. Such a subject is called a step-wedge, and so the process of determining exposure may be called wedging. When shooting the test it is advisable to fix all variable elements except one at the theoretical "mean" exposure; the one variable – most easily the lens iris – should be moved through a range from about one stop below to one stop above the anticipated "mean" position.

Divide the distance between *f* stops into at least two, or even four sections to produce extremely subtle changes. Table one frame at each setting. You need careful notes of the procedure so that when you examine the test after processing you know exactly what setting gave the right exposure. If you anticipate several different set-ups, make a test at each, so that you can be sure of what you are doing.

It is also wise to shoot a grey scale at the head of each cartridge under the standard conditions for the "mean" exposure. If you get a cartridge back from processing with a different-looking grey scale, you may be able to find a laboratory to print the whole cartridge with adjustments to match the grey scale to your normal result.

Colour chart

A grey scale gives an indication of the full reproduction of tonal values. Also, under normal conditions, any colour irregularities will also become apparent in the form of an overall colour cast. With perfect colour reproduction the grey scale is truly black, grey and white. This of course is not always possible in practice. The variation of the density of the film produced by a variation in exposure can make considerable changes in the way colour is reproduced. For this purpose and to determine the precise effect the colour cast may have on specific colour, you can use a colour chart.

However, the more serious threat to the colour reproduction lies not so much in the inaccurate exposure as in the colour temperature of the light (see page 122). You can make a certain amount of colour correction (and indeed deliberate colour distortions) with filters, either over the light source or over the camera lens. For this, you are best advised to go through the same procedure as in the case of the grey scale. Establish the desired effect by means of a test, on which you vary the exposure, frame by frame. You need to do this with every filter combination because each one has a different absorption factor. (See page 128.)

Exposure meters

You measure intensity with a light meter, or exposure meter. One scientific measure is foot-candles. However most of the scales used by manufacturers do not in fact refer to foot candles. They refer directly to exposure values or f-stops. A simplification which was probably unnecessary.

Apart from measuring the intensity of the light, an exposure meter is equipped with a series of scales which enable the user to "compute" the exposure based on the light reading obtained. This is done by means of finding a suitable correlation between exposure time, and f-stop for a specific film speed.

Reflected light readings are the most common. That is, the majority of light meters measure the intensity of light reflected by the subject being photographed. This is generally quite acceptable — but there are very many occasions where this method is likely to give the wrong kind of indication. Problems come when the acceptance angle of the light meter is not the same as that of the camera lens; or the emphasis between the light and the dark areas are not in proportion.

Imagine a puppet at the entrance of a dark cave as seen from the inside.

Clearly a light reading from the camera point of view will result in the over-exposure of the key area of interest because the meter gives equal importance to the dark walls of the cave as to the light area around the puppet. The best solution in this case is to take the reading from the puppet only. An additional reading of the background gives a useful guide to the contrast ratio between the dark and light areas. Of course, that must not be too great if any detail is to be reproduced in the dark areas. If you are in any doubt, take a reading from a uniform grey card in the subject position. Follow that for optimum reproductions of the entire range of tones. You can do that too, for flat artwork with unusual contrasts.

An *incident light reading* measures the intensity of the light falling on the subject. For the computation of exposure, this reading is roughly equivalent to the reflected light reading off a grey card. This is much better than reflected light metering for maintaining consistency of exposure. However, for the best results it is always advisable to use both methods.

The incident light reading is done through a translucent white cone fitted to the light meter. The meter is held close to the subject with the cone facing the camera. The meter should be perpendicular to the lens axis so that the light hits the cone at roughly the same angle that it falls on the subject.

Problems with automatic metering

Most 8 mm cameras are equipped with light measuring devices. Often they are linked to the film speed setting, exposure time and the iris. This way the exposure is set automatically. The method may have some dubious advantages in live action shooting at continuous speeds, but it is most undesirable for animation shooting.

Imagine our earlier example of the puppet outside the cave being shot in this way. Suppose the shot was to start with a close-up of the fully lit subject and then zoom out to the wide angle taking in the unlit cave. The change in exposure (which would be done automatically) would destroy the shot totally. It is absolutely vital to use manual override if such undesirable changes in exposure are to be avoided.

A built-in meter can still be used as a conventional light meter giving reflected light readings. You can check carefully selected sections of the scene using the zoom to give a narrow angle. Combined with a judicious use of a grey card, you can produce extremely goods results.

Lighting

There may be some practical operational advantages when using 8 mm gauge arising out of its compactness compared to the professional 35 mm gauge. But when it comes to lighting, the requirements are much the same. This is because the sensitivity (speed) of the colour emulsions and the exposure times are much the same. To obtain the best results, you need plenty of light for flat artwork animation. This requirement is essentially limited to two fairly powerful lamps.

When it comes to the animation of solid objects your needs can range from one to a whole battery of lights – depending on the size of the set and the needs of specific shots. As a general rule of thumb a stronger (and this does not necessarily mean bigger) light source is preferable to a weaker one. It is always easy to cut down the intensity of the light to the required level but it is impossible to increase it from an inadequate source.

Colour temperature

In ensuring the true colour reproduction of a scene there is one key factor that needs to be given due attention – that is the colour

121

temperature of the light source. Visible light, i.e. the radiation seen by the human eye, is made of up electromagnetic particles travelling at different frequencies within a specific range. A mixture of all this visible range is seen as "white light". You can pass it through a refracting element to separate each different frequency into a solid band of colour – i.e. the colour spectrum as seen in the rainbow.

When white light falls onto a surface, a certain proportion of it is absorbed and the rest is reflected. The absorption-reflection ratio varies from one type of surface to another; and what is more important it does not affect all the frequencies in equal proportion. Some surfaces absorb most of the frequencies and reflect only those of one colour. For example, if it absorbs all but those in the red band, we then see that surface as being red in colour.

The electromagnetic frequencies are described by wavelengths. For example deepest purple is 385 nanometers and the deepest red is 750 nanometers. The nanometre (nm) is one thousand millionth of a meter.

Colour film emulsion is made up of three layers. Each is sensitive to a specific group of wavelengths, with overlaps so that between them they cover the visible spectrum. Basically there is one layer sensitive to each of blue, green and red light. So white light affects each layer in exactly the same way. Average daylight has more-or-less equal quantities of each wavelength. So, colour emulsions for daylight use have more-or-less equal sensitivities to each wavelength. Other sources produce light with different proportions. Light from a tungsten filament contains a much higher proportion of long-wavelength radiation (i.e. red). So film for such illumination needs to be less red-sensitive. If you use that film in daylight, it produces a blue coloured bias.

The colour temperature of average daylight is around 5600 K. K here stands for Kelvin and represents the scale used for measuring the colour temperature of light. The colour temperature of most artifical lights is much lower than that of daylight – and, what is more important, it varies. Because of this, a standard colour temperature was chosen and most photographic lamps intended for colour photography are made to this specification: it is 3200 K.

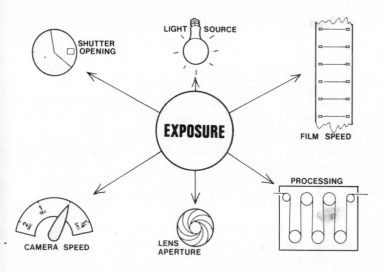

2.

1, Factors involved in determining the exposure. 2, A typical high contrast situation where automatic metering is unsuitable.

Professional movie type film stocks are balanced for 3200 K, but most 8 mm films are made for 3400 K. So you need lights that produce 3400 K, such as photoflood bulbs or movie lights. Studio lights for still work often produce 3200 K. They will then produce a slightly warm tinge on super-8 colour film.

Even when you have the right lamp, the voltage can be a serious contributory factor to any changes in the colour temperature. So, if you have any doubt, make sure that the voltage is always the same when you shoot your animation.

Correcting the colour temperature

Colour temperature can be measured with a colour temperature meter, but these are rather expensive. If you stick to the lights of the prescribed colour temperature and use a compatible emulsion, there is no need to have a colour temperature meter of your own. To achieve perfect results, though, you must entertain a certain amount of colour correction, because neither colour emulsions nor light bulbs are always absolutely accurate. The tolerances are acceptable by most standards. You make corrections with colour correction filters. To decide exactly what you want, the procedure is much the same as exposure "wedging" (see page 116). Just as the exposure is gradually altered frame by frame between predetermined points so the colour is changed with a series of slightly increasing density (strength). If you are rephotographing a distinctly off-colour transparency, you can do a certain amount of colour correction purely visually. Hold colour correction filters over the transparency until you see which one makes the desired improvement. It is advisable for this, to have some sort of reference, such as a transparency of a colour-chart or other well exposed and well balanced transparency, because the eye can be deceived.

The wrong type of light

Virtually all super-8 colour film is type A, i.e. balanced for exposure in artificial (3400 K) lighting. If you use 3200 K lights, you will get slightly "warmer" results. You can correct this with a pale blue filter (such as a Wratten 82A). However, if you are shooting *all* your work with 3200 K lighting, you will probably be quite happy without a filter. The slight warmth of colour only shows if you mix with normally shot material.

Super-8 cameras have a filter built in to let you shoot on the type A material in daylight. This is in place unless you remove it. Many models have an accessory light mounting. When you mount a "movie light", or a substitute key, the filter is removed. Other cameras have a switch. Make sure that you switch out the filter whenever you shoot in artifical light — and put it back for any daylight shots.

With other cameras, you must fit your own filter for daylight shooting with artificial light film or vice versa.

The governing factor must always be the film emulsion. If the emulsion is balanced for daylight, and one of the elements has to be shot in artificial light then a conversion filter is used in front of the lens. This filter is blue in colour and is known as a daylight to artificial conversion filter, such as the Kodak Wratten filter No. 80B (which reduces film speed by $1\frac{2}{3}$ stop). Alternatively, blue filters can be used over the lights.

For the other way round, an artificial (tungsten) to daylight conversion filter is used, such as a Kodak Wratten filter No. 85 or 85B (it reduces film speed by $\frac{2}{3}$ of a stop).

Mixing light sources

When daylight and artificial light have to be used at the same time, then the blue filters are added to the lights for daylight film. If artificial lights have to be mixed with daylight while shooting on artificial light emulsion, then the salmon coloured conversion filter (the one fitted to all super-8 cameras) is still used, with blue filters on the lights. In those exceptional cases where, for example, you may have a puppet on a window sill looking out into the garden, it may become practical to light the puppet without using blues on lights, the conversion filter is also dispensed with on the lens and instead a larger sheet of the same salmon coloured filter (gelatine as supplied for light) is then placed on the window glass. Naturally all other daylight should be eliminated from the room unless it is also filtered in the same way.

Filter holders

Lamps can often be fitted with flaps (barn doors) which are used to prevent the light reaching certain areas of the scene. When it is necessary to use filters these are usually clipped onto these flaps for support. This is a very untidy arrangement but unfortunately it is used extensively, because it works. A much better arrangement is to make filter holders which are attached to the front of the light in place of the flaps. Since most conventional light sources emit much radiation in the invisible range of the spectrum (i.e. heat) as in the visible one (light) these filter holders should be mounted some distance from the lamp's face. Additionally there should be free air circulating between the filters and the lamp. The section which actually holds the filters is of a box-like construction and can be made of wood (it is advisable to line the wood with asbestos at the point of contact with the metal supports). It is divided into several sections so that it can accommodate more than one filter at a time.

The filters materials themselves are framed on rectangular supports which fit easily into the cutout of the holder. A series of standard filters such as Neutral Density, diffusion filters, e.g. spun glass, wires, ground glass and gauzes, as well as some strong basic colours can all be prepared in advance and used as and when required. You should try to keep one or two filter supports clear for any new requirements.

The size of the filter holder depends largely on the width of beam-spread and how close can a 'gelatine' filter be placed for a reasonable length of time without burning.

Filters

N.D. Filters are used to reduce the intensity of a light source without altering the colour in any way. They come in various strengths and can be obtained for specific use on lights (they are not the same optical quality as those commonly used in front of the camera lens and are consequently a lot cheaper). With a series of these filters in the strengths of 0.3 (one *f* stop) and 0.6 (2 *f* stops) most combinations of other strengths can be obtained. (0.1 and 0.2 are also useful for finger gradations, but they are generally available only in small sizes for use as lens filters).

Diffusion filters are used to diffuse the light, i.e. make it much softer. With greater diffusion, the shadows become less apparent and one of the prime uses of diffused light is to act as a shadow killer. Also, many glossy surfaces require diffused lighting to avoid glare.

Diffusion can also be achieved by bouncing (reflecting) the light off a white card before it reaches the subject, but the degree of control over this method is not as great as directing a suitably diffused light source directly at the subject. Virtually any translucent material can serve as a diffuser — grease-proof paper, ground glass, opal plastic, glass etc. Unfortunately any diffuser also absorbs a lot of light itself. Spun glass is a fibre glass material produced for just this sort of purpose and it has probably the best diffusion/absorption characteristics. A special wire mesh is also a very good diffuser. In fact, even ordinary wire mesh is quite good. The result is a patchy, patterned diffusion which can give a very good effect on a roughly textured surface. Gauses also produce this kind of effect.

When it is necessary to increase the diffusion, then you can use several layers of the diffusion material or a combination of materials. The most important consideration in choosing the diffusion material is to avoid altering the colour of the light. So never use anything with a noticeable colour.

Basic colour filters are useful for changing the overall colour bias of a specific section of a scene and particularly useful for lighting three-dimensional sets. For example, you can produce a dramatic red glow on the horizon with light from a strong red filter bounced off the backdrop. Many other dramatic lighting effects are possible with a careful accentuation of a colour in one specific area of the scene. The most useful colours for this purpose are blue and orange, although most other colours can be used effectively in the right setting.

It must be remembered that all filters absorb a certain amount of light: the stronger the colour, the greater the absorption. It is therefore necessary to know the filter factor of the specific filter in use in order to determine the light loss. However, with time filters collect dust and may in fact transmit less light than the filter factors suggests and the light meter is the only reliable guide.

Masking filters are made up of shapes cut out of black opaque paper which is supported on the filter frame. They serve to prevent the light from reaching certain areas in the scene, like the original flaps on the lamp. There is, though, one major difference – they can be infinitely more accurate. You can cut specific shapes and patterns to create just the effect you want on the scene.

The edges of the shadows cast are graduated (soft) and can be made even more so with the additional use of diffusers. Matching male–female masks on two different lights can produce a lighting effect of even intensity over a scene with perceptable alterations from one colour to the other. Whirling patterns of colour in the background can be produced with the use of one or two lights and masking filters with small shapes cut out at random; filter patches of various colours can be placed over each cutout shape separately and the two lamps are then moved, frame by frame, in opposite directions.

In flat artwork animation, masking filters are particularly useful for creating vignetting effects to make a certain section of the area photographed appear to stand out from the rest (masking filter on one light – no filter on the other); or to make that area be seen in normal colour while the surrounding area has a distinct colour bias as well as being darker (a complementary masking filter and a colour filter). The complementary 'male' masking filter as in the last example can be stuck to another filter that may be in use or else it has to be supported on a piece of clear glass.

Polarising filters

A set of polarising filters is absolutely essential for shooting animation – particularly the flat artwork type. These filters do not just
help to eliminate virtually all glare, they also help with the
problems of dust particles and other blemishes that may be
gathered by the artwork during the shooting. A good quality clear
glass can be used over the artwork to keep it flat without any
dangers of undesirable reflections. When glossy surfaces (and
objects made of glass and other materials that tend to produce a
glare) are photographed as part of a solid set then the use of
polarising filters can save hours of diddling with lights to avoid the
glare.

Polarisation

As we have seen earlier, the light is made of electromagnetic particles travelling at high frequencies. Each ray moves in one particular direction away from the light source; but the light vibrates
in all directions around the axis of travel. Polarising materials
possess properties which permit the light particles vibrating only in
one specific plane to pass through, while the others are absorbed.
Put a sheet of polarising material in front of a light source and the
light passing through it becomes polarised; i.e. the light rays are all
vibrating in one plane. If another piece of polarising material is
placed in this light path with its polarisation axis matching that of
the first polariser, the light will pass through virtually unobstructed.
If the second polariser is rotated so that its polarising axis now lies
at 90° to that of the first polariser, theoretically no light will be able
to pass through.
Light can also be polarised by reflection. When the sun rays fall on
highly reflective surfaces they become polarised. This is why in
normal exterior photography a polarising filter on the lens can
reduce some reflections drastically. Already polarised light remains
polarised if it is reflected specularly (as in a shiny surface). It loses
its polarisation if its is scattered from a normal matte surface.

In animation reflections are suppressed by placing a polarising screen over the light sources as well as over the camera lens. So, all the light is polarised in the same plane before it reaches the artwork. It is most important that all lights are polarised, and that the axes of polarisation (indicated on the filter in the form of an arrow) are parallel.

The easiest way is to line up all the filters either horizontal or vertical, regardless of the angles of tilt at which the lights will be used. The lens polariser is always placed in front of the lens with its polarising axis at 90° to that of the light's screens. That way, the film is exposed only by the light scattered from the artwork. Any specularly reflected light is absorbed by the filter over the camera lens.

The lens filter holder, as well as the ones on the lights should be at fixed positions so that the relationship between the polarising axis remains the same. This is of extreme importance because any small deviation can produce considerable changes in the exposure.

Quality and choice of polarisers

The lens polariser should be of "movie" quality, preferably mounted in glass. It should also ideally be the same type as the light screens (which can be bought as plastic sheets cut to the desired size). When deciding on the size of the filter holder it should be remembered that polarising screens are rather expensive; equally they should not be exposed to great heat for any lengths of time.

They come in different strengths; the weakest ones absorb least light but they are also least efficient. The really strong ones are extremely efficient but are not truly neutral in colour, and so may alter colour temperature of the light. Further, they produce an increase in contrast which is not acceptable for conventional photography. The most suitable is type H.N. 38. The total loss of light with a set of this type fully "crossed" is in the region of 3 stops. So if your exposure without filters on either the lights or the lens requires $f11$, it will be $f4$ with H.N. 38 polarisers. It is best to

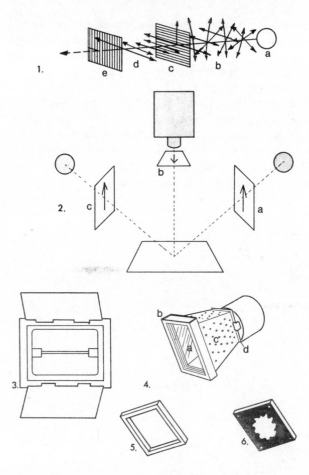

1, How polarizers work. (a) Light source. (b) Light particles vibrating in all directions. (c) Polarizing screen with a horizontal axis of polarization. (d) Vibration in the vertical plane only. (e) A polarizing screen with a vertical polarization axis absorbs horizontal polarized light.

2, With suitably crossed polarizers on lights and lens, you can shoot shiny artwork with no reflections.

3, Light source with barn doors. 4, Filter holder fitted to the lamp in place of barn doors (a) filter, (b) opening, (c) cooling holes, (d) mounting frame. 5, A blank filter mount which slides into the holder. 6, Cut-out mask.

determine your own exposure under each set of specific conditions you use and enter the details on the exposure chart for future reference.

A certain increase in the contrast is characteristic of all polarisers, but in the case of H.N. 38 this increase is not very great and if anything, it tends to improve the definition in the artwork. You can produce really black areas with such filters — particularly from *glossy* black surfaces. This is used deliberately for superimpositions. Lettering, for example, can be made to stand out clearly on a background which does not in fact photograph at all and so does not affect the already exposed image.

Lighting for Animation

Two lights are used for lighting flat artwork. They are positioned on each side of the camera so that the camera and the animation set up can always be easily approached from the front. Make sure that the lights do not restrict the movements of the table in any way. It is best to suspend them on brackets from the back wall or to have them on free standing supports independent from the animation table, yet firmly fixed.

Line up procedure

It is important to establish the largest field size first. This is the largest area on the shooting table which has to be lit evenly. Outline this field size on the table, draw vertical and horizontal lines through the centre – the centre should align with the position of the lens centre. It is the same for all smaller field sizes.

Put the lamps directly opposite each other at equal distances from the centre and along an extention of the horizontal line. Move them away from the table to the point where the width of each light beam fully covers the largest field size, when it is directed at the centre. The angle at which the light reaches the table top is also going to depend largely on this distance. But, don't make it too shallow, because then you are more likely to produce shadows of the upper layers of artwork on the lower ones; particularly in cel and cutout animation. Also, the eliptical shape of the beam is more pronounced. On the other hand, a very steep angle produces reflection problems and can be awkard when using a shadow board and all the effects associated with it. (Particularly in the case of set ups which rely on tracking the camera instead of using a zoom lens.) The most convenient angles are between 35° and 45° to the horizontal.

If both lights are positioned at the same distance from the field centre and at the same height from the horizontal, and also both tilted down in the same way, the incident light reading at the lens centre should be the same for each light. The lights should always be checked individually in this way before the joint reading is taken. Because of the eliptical shape of the light beams, there is a certain unevenness which is corrected by the opposite light. When both lights are on, you can check the entire area of the largest field size for evenness of illumination. Check the line up frequently to ensure both the correct light level and the evenness of the spread. If the lights have spotting and flooding facilities, use this for alignment. Set them to give the narrowest beam of light, which can then easily be directed at the lens centre mark on the shooting table. This way the lights can be checked quickly and brought back into correct alignment. Once aligned, then set them both at full flood position again for shooting.

Lighting solid objects on flat artwork

Occasionally, small solid objects need to be incorporated into a scene which consists mainly of flat artwork. For example, you might want to use a pencil, rubber, various small geometric shapes, coins, etc. The cross lighting which is normally used for flat artwork produces a double shadow of the solid object which is most disturbing. You must do something, if you eliminate the shadows altogether, you would lose the impression of solidity.

It is best to move one of the lights to a new position (or use an additional light) and making it the "key" light which will produce the one desirable shadow. The length of this shadow is determined by the angle of incidence. The other light of the standard set up can be used as a fill light with appropriate diffusion filters placed upon it. This light must not be so bright as to produce a strong secondary shadow but at the same time it must be bright enough to illuminate the artwork. Take great care in the setting up of the key light to ensure that the entire field size is evenly lit, and that any fall off from the second light is fully compensated.

Backlight

Backlight is necessary for silhouette animation and the photography of transparencies. In its most basic form it may consist of a simple light box. Be sure that the colour temperature of the light is correct, particularly when photographing transparencies. If the light box is small enough, it can sometimes be carried on the animation table so that a certain amount of movement becomes possible, although this system has inherent limitations.

If you have a slightly more sophisticated animation compound then it is wise to provide for a cutout area in the middle which can serve as a window for backlight. A piece of clear glass is placed over the opening, so that its upper surface is level with the top of the table. This glass serves to support backlit artwork, but can be left in position for top-lit shooting also. This way the backlit artwork can have the full benefit of all the movements which are possible on your compound.

The light source

Of course, your light source is positioned below the shooting table. The farther from the table surface, the bigger the area it can cover. If it is too close to the table surface it can restrict the movements of the compound. If it is too far, it may not be bright enough.

You can use a light placed at the bottom of the table and directed upwards. For this, you have to replace the clear glass with a good diffuser such as an opal glass (or plastic) or ground glass. However there are two distinct disadvantages to this system: the diffusers are always in the position of the primary focus of the lens so that their texture and graininess tend to be noticeable – particularly in the clear areas such as the sky in a transparency. Secondly heat built up in the diffuser is easily transmitted to the artwork. One way around this problem is to place the diffusers at a certain distance from the plane of primary focus (table top) so that their texture becomes less noticeable because the grains are out of focus, clear glass can then be left in the table cutout to support the artwork, and the gap between the diffusers and the artwork provides increased ventilation.

However, the simplest way of producing a soft, even backlight quickly is to use a sheet of white card and fix it below the shooting table at 45° to the lens axis. Mount a lamp close to the floor so that the light bounces off the white card towards the artwork.

Alternatively, the white card (or better still a wooden board with a white formica surface) can be placed horizontally below the animation table. Two or more light sources are used to bounce light off this white surface and provide even, diffused backlight.

Blacking out

It is most important to black out around the animation compound to prevent the light scattering. Apart from undesirable reflections the presence of any other light in the room can wash out the image which is meant to be lit only from behind. Black, opaque cloth is ideal for this purpose. Fix it to the machinery or to a suitable frame.

Lighting for the animation of solid objects

The basic principle in lighting solid objects is to try and simulate natural conditions. A great deal depends on the setting, and it is this setting as well as particular dramatic requirements that should give the clue to the lighting. For example, if the set represents a room with a large window, then the light for that room would be coming through the window in a real room. So, we should also use the window as the key source of light. This can vary a great deal from a very strong light streaming in and projecting clearly defined shadows, to a much more diffused light as on a dull day. Then the interior of the room is lit mainly by diffused bounced light producing faint shadows.

If a lamp within a set is meant to be on, then that should also be exploited as another source of light in the room and suitably emphasised. Remember that the answer is not in simply flooding the set with light to make sure that every corner is exposed correctly. Don't be afraid of the dark corners and bright spots if that is what a place might look like in real life. It is the shadow that makes the picture by giving it contours – the light only helps to expose the film.

The same guidelines apply when the set is meant to represent an exterior. In bright sunshine there is only one dominant shadow . . . but when the day is overcast, the lighting is diffused. At night there is even more scope; apart from the moon giving a strong shadow, there can be a lot of light sources to accentuate dramatically – such as brightly lit windows and street lamps. For the best effect these highlights should be made to appear isolated in a sea of blackness in which only the outlines of other parts of the set are visible.

If you use abstract backgrounds, the light can play an even greater role. A couple of geometric shapes and a drape can be made to reflect a variety of moods with the use of carefully positioned lights and colour filters.

Basic principles

In most cases the lighting of solid objects calls for the use of more than one light source. Point several lights at your set more-or-less at random and, inevitably, there are likely to be just as many different shadows of the objects as the number of light sources. Whatever other unrealistic lighting results are possible – this is certainly the most noticeable and least acceptable of all. On the other hand a completely diffused lighting, (which in any case is not the easiest thing in the world to achieve on a small set) certainly cannot be appropriate for all scenes. Whatever the scene, the basic principles revolves around the establishment of only one shadow – as in the case of bright sunlight, produced by the "key" light.

The key light

Sometimes, of course, the scene demands more than one key light in one set; but the subject should be positioned so that only *one* of them does in fact produce a visible shadow. When the subject is moved nearer to the second key light, the shadow produced by this light should be allowed to predominate. Let us, though, discuss only the single key light, appropriate to most settings.

The positioning of this is of extreme importance. The main clue as to the direction and the angle of the key light must be gleaned from the set and the script requirements. Still, you must take account of other factors, especially those largely connected with continuity. Because the key light cannot be changed during a shot, it is best to go through all the possible angles that may be needed with that specific lighting before establishing the precise positioning of the key-light. With puppets, look at all their key positions on the set to ensure that they don't throw shadows onto each other and that they are all lit reasonably with the key light at that particular position. For larger sets, you may need several lamps to produce the single key light to cover the whole scene.

Fill light

With key lighting alone, the shadows will be much too dark. You use a diffused light to "fill in" the shadow areas. It provides overall illumination for the whole set. The fill must be of lower intensity than the key light so that it does not create a secondary shadow. In practice, you probably need several lights to produce a sufficiently diffused fill-in over a wider area.

Skylight is an additional fill light which can sometimes be used to increase the general level of luminosity of the whole scene. It consists of one or more diffused lights suspended directly above the set, acting much the same as the sky in the real exteriors.

Backlight

Lighting from behind the subject is often referred to as modelling or effect light, because its main function is to isolate an object

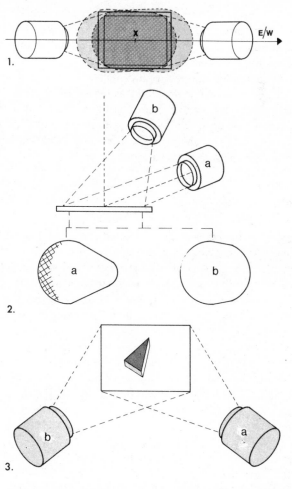

1, For even lighting, each light gives the same reading when measured separately at the table centre (x). 2, Small angles of incidence (a) produce rather uneven lighting over the full area of the table. Steeper angles (b) produce even more spread, but it is still uneven and is compensated by the second light directly opposite and set at the same angle.

3, When lighting solid objects, one light – the "key" (a) is brighter than the other – the "fill" (b).

from the background. It is placed directly behind the subject and is usually carefully masked off so as to fall on the subject only and to avoid spilling over onto unwanted areas. The position of this light is not fixed for a particular lighting setup and is governed by the positions of the figures because it is mainly the figures which are lit in this way to give them a greater feeling of depth. Because these figures move about the set, the backlight may require the use of more than one lamp. Each is set for specific positions in the action. These lamps are generally positioned relatively high to avoid the light spilling onto the camera lens.

"Contra-jour" effect

On occasions the key light can be a backlight in the same way you can shoot against the sun in a real situation. This approach should be reserved for very special occasions when it is really justified by the content of the story. The effect creates a halo of light around the figure or figures and the extent of this halo depends on the contrast ratio between the shadow area illuminated by the fill light and the backlight. Two different effects are in fact possible with different exposures. Base your exposure reading of the areas lit by the fill light, ignoring the strong backlight completely; you get a very pronounced halo effect on a pastel coloured scene. A much more dramatic effect results if you stop down the exposure by one and a half or two stops. You get large dark areas broken up by the highlights of the halo. This is particularly useful when lighting for a moonlight or general night effect. It is particularly spectacular where your solid subjects are suitably textured.

Contrast ratio

The secret of good lighting lies in the contrast ratio between the key light and the fill light. The human eye has a much wider range of tonal perception than the film emulsion — particularly colour reversal film. This means that the eye can see detail in the dark areas of a brightly lit scene which are simply photographed as black by the film emulsion. It is because of this that judging the lighting of a scene with an untrained eye can produce disappointments.

A colour contrast viewing filter helps with a visual check. Only a small amount of light passes through this filter so that the luminance range is effectively compressed to correspond roughly to that of the film emulsion. In practice a very strong neutral density filter will do just as well. Contrast ratio can be appreciated more easily in black and white terms than in colour – it can also be judged more easily this way. The use of the viewing filter has the added benefit that the scene can be appreciated more in terms of tones, although all colours are not completely lost. The reason for this is that the human eye has two sets of receptors in the retina which transfer the impulses to the brain. These are cones (sensitive to the full range of colours) and rods which are more sensitive but colour blind because they interpret light in terms of black and white tones only. At very low light levels it is the rods that come into play more than cones and the perception of colour becomes compressed with the result that a red or blue shirt looks black at dusk.

Because the eye can be so easily deceived, it is best to rely on aids such as the light meter to give you the precise ratio between the light sources. For best results, and unless you want a particular effect, the ratio between the key light and the fill light should be around 2:1.

In calculating the ratios, measure the light sources separately either as incident readings or reflected readings from a grey card; the relative position of the camera is not important. You must, though measure the light as near the subject as is convenient. Be especially careful with small subjects; it is sometimes difficult to measure from exactly the right place. The camera or stand may throw a shadow on the meter or on the grey card. Obviously, if that is so, you will not get a time reading.

The next stage is to establish the necessary exposure level. Having established the desired contrast ratio, take an exposure reading with both key and fill lights on. Of course, the camera position must be taken into account for the calculation of the exposure. Because the reflecting properties of the set are likely to vary, it is necessary to take this into account also. A reflected reading can be taken of the shadow areas and compared with highlights.

Shot Planning

Pre-production

A certain amount of preproduction work is advisable, even when you think you know precisely what you want to achieve. It helps to clarify the best way of achieving your goal and can help you avoid certain problems that you might otherwise overlook. Naturally, scripting forms the key part of this preproduction work and it goes without saying that the idea and the script come first.

Because film making is such a visual art form (particularly animation), the ideas in the script have to be expressed visually also before the actual production is undertaken. For this, you make a story board. A story board is a series of rough sketches of the key situations predicting the progress of a scene. Various camera moves, framing of the action, and timings can be represented in this way and studied before the artwork is prepared. So, you can avoid possible snags and select the best and most effective angles. Story boards are equally important for flat artwork and solid object animation. Establish a scale chart indicating the relative sizes of the characters and colour reference charts — before the work proper begins so that you can maintain continuity. The continuity of picture quality is just as important as the continuity of the action which is depicted on the storyboard.

If you are working on flat artwork, you can try out a character or movement on a "flicker book". Just draw each key stage *in register* on succeeding sheets of paper. Hold the paper together with one hand while you flick through the pages with the other. So you see each page in turn. Flick reasonably quickly, and the animation happens. With a bit of practice, you can maintain a nice even flicker rate. Then you can judge the relative timing of the various stages in your animation sequence.

Shot keys

Shot keys are used in flat artwork animation to indicate the framing for a particular shot. Take a piece of semi-transparent paper (copy paper, grease-proof paper) which is punched in the same way as the artwork for registration purposes and draw on it the field size. For this, you need a framing device, such as a graticule or two L shaped pieces of card. A graticule consists of a series of rectangular shapes of the same proportions as camera aperture engraved on an acetate cell at regular intervals (usually 1 in) all having one common centre.

Later, you place the shot key over the finished artwork, so that you can line up the camera to the outline without any further worries. The shot key is particularly useful when camera moves are involved, because it helps you to make up your mind as to the precise framing at the start and the end of each move before you get on the camera. This is where directing is really done because the shot key gives a clear indication of what the shot will look like. If you don't like the look of the shot you only have to do another key and you will not have wasted a lot of film stock and effort. A certain amount of shot planning can be done when the artwork is outlined — before it is fully painted; this way certain areas beyond a safe margin can be left unpainted.

Measurement of pans

Mark the centres of each rectangle (representing each stage of the shot). There will be just two rectangles for a straightforward pan. The distance between their centres is the distance of the pan and can be used for any preliminary calculations to arrive at the constant increment for each frame of the shot. The distance is simply divided by the number of frames representing the length of the move in time. When the centres are joined up, the distance between them can be indicated along the line. Of course, it is at this stage that you must consider all the other factors, such as strobing, and adjust the shot as necessary.

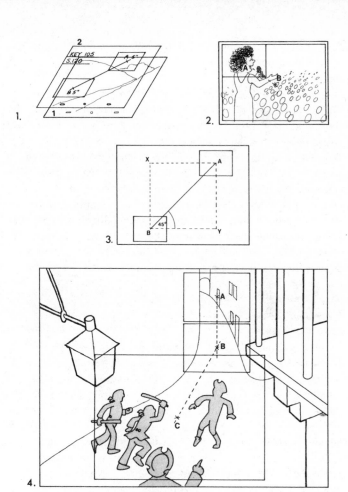

Shot planning. 1, A shot key and artwork. 3, 45° pans. A diagonal pan at 45° needs the same east-west and north-south movements (AX and BY). Constant increments and fairings will be the same for both.

Artistic considerations. 2, Where the perspective is right, a zoom out from a field size can be very effective. 4, A vertical pan down a narrow street sets the mood without the perspective being too clear at this field size. A sudden pull out (to position c) appears as though the camera had been tilted down – due to the high angle of the perspective in the full drawing.

A zoom is measured in terms of the difference between the field sizes and is represented by the amount the zoom ring has to be rotated or the actual distance the camera is tracked. The distance between the centres of the start and finish rectangles represents the exact amount of pan that may be needed for any particular zoom-and-pan shot. When calculating the move these two elements are considered separately.

When drawing up a shot key you are thinking in terms of conventional moves (where it is the camera which actually moves). This can produce some confusion when you actually start shooting (particularly if you are working upside down as well) because it is really the artwork that moves and the camera that stays fixed. It is advisable to indicate the centres of each rectangle as A, B, C etc.; which gives a clear indication where the shot begins, and where it ends (with all other key intermediate positions).

Technical considerations

Careful anticipation of all shooting problems can save you a lot of unnecessary effort. As we have seen in an earlier chapter the lengths of pans can be manipulated by alterations in the field sizes to accommodate extra frames when calculating fairings for the various moves. In the case of diagonal moves, the angle of the pan in relation to the horizontal can be altered slightly to give a convenient working ratio between East-West and North-South moves. It must be remembered that it is the distance of the horizontal and vertical moves that is compared to obtain a convenient ratio. If you can make a diagonal move with one panning move only, the artwork is pegged so that its horizontal is at the correct angle to the direction of travel of the movement for that specific diagonal pan. The key then makes it easy not only to line up to the correct field size positions but also to show just where rotation needs to be set. This of course, is done by simply making sure that the horizontal and vertical outlines of the rectangles indicated on the shot-key are matched to the framelines projected through the camera (for this, you use the rotoscope, see page 105).

Artistic considerations

Shot planning involves the selection of frames that are complete pictures in themselves, although they may in fact form part of a larger picture. It is important to think in terms of pictures within pictures and then what kind of camera moves suggest themselves to connect these key frames. Very often a move may not be appropriate at all and the film works better with a quick static cut. It is not necessary to show the entire picture either — this is particularly relevant when you are dealing with existing artwork such as picture postcards and photographs.

Don't be afraid to select only one particular area or pan across another when it is appropriate. The obligation some people feel in showing the entire picture leads to the inevitable static wide shots or constant zooming in or out. Framing plays such an important part in this selection of key points of interest within a larger picture. A geometrically even frame is not necessarily a good frame. This is particularly true of profiles — where it is always better to have a certain amount of room in front of the face and crop the back of the head than to have the nose at the edge of the frame and the ear in the centre. It is the centre of interest within the subject which must be made to dominate the frame.

Sympathetic moves

When deciding on the camera moves it is important to choose moves which are in sympathy with the picture. Perspective plays a great part in this and should be given a lot of consideration. You can paint pictures with false perspectives, so that as the camera pans from one point of interest to another it appears as though the camera angle has changed. The choice of the camera move should also be governed by the soundtrack or the storyline, for a camera move can be absolutely beautiful and at the same time totally inappropriate within the context that it is used. When shooting to music only, there are certain musical phrases which suggest specific camera moves, i.e. they are in sympathy with each other.

147

The extreme example of the wrong ideas would be to use whip pans and crash zooms over a slow pastoral piece of music – however appropriate the artwork itself may be, or to use slow, drifting pans over a pounding disco number.

Animation table

Shot planning is usually done on an animation table. In its simplest form this can be just a board with registration pegs to register the artwork with. Moving pegbars (top and bottom) in a rotating ring can give all the possible movements of the camera compound and are obviously much more useful. A light built into the table can illuminate a piece of ground glass set in the central area for use with backlit artwork and transparencies during shot planning as well as for the preparation of artwork (tracing and painting in particular).

If you build your own camera table, you can make the compound movable. Then you can use that for shot planning and artwork preparation without the camera and lights getting in the way.

Dope sheets

Shot keys have all the information required regarding the start and end of particular moves during the shot, but the length of those moves in frames (time) as well as the length of the pauses at the start and the end of each move is indicated on a separate sheet of paper which carries all other camera instruction. This is the dope sheet. The dope sheet also indicates all the animation changes during, and in-between, the moves.

Where there are not a lot of changes in the artwork, the dope can take the simple form of about five columns to indicate the background, and cell layers 1 to 4. The starting set up is indicated and the camera instructions then follow until the point for the change in the artwork is reached. A mix or cut are indicated and then the artwork set up is entered again incorporating the desired change in a particular layer, and so on. Where no animation changes occur in the artwork, the camera moves for a whole series of shots can be incorporated on the same dope sheet so that a complete sequence can be shot without a break, and therefore without the need for any editing. The editing is in fact done in the camera (or to be more precise, at the shot-planning stage). This is particularly useful for sequences designed to go with specific pieces of music. On the other hand when a lot of animation is used (e.g. cartoons) a very much more detailed dope sheet is necessary to allow for changes in the artwork for every frame if necessary, as well as camera movements simultaneous with animation.

Dope sheets are also prepared for cutout animation and puppet animation although they serve more as guides to the animator and don't have to be adhered to with the absolute accuracy demanded by most flat artwork animation.

Timings

The dope sheets are based on the timings which are arrived at by a careful study of movement and a visualisation of the shot. A stop watch is useful, but timing an animation shot is done by visualising the shot and the movement in the mind and then translating that into real time – i.e. number of frames. Don't be afraid to get up and walk like your character or to make wild gestures that may help you to arrive at the right timings for those moves – just make sure no one sees you.

Sound breakdown

If narration or dialogue is going to be included in your film, then you can time each sentence with a stop watch to give a reasonable approximation of the pace – provided you make a point of reading it aloud in the same way as it will be recorded later. However, for any animation, it is best to pre-record the soundtrack before the artwork is done – either as single items or sequences. You can even complete the whole film in sound only first. You then take accurate timings from the recording. This is sound breakdown. Even lip-sync is possible for the real masochist. Those slightly less ambitious can begin with the breakdown of their favourite piece of music and shooting suitable visuals to go with it — it can be a very rewarding experience. It is important though to start with a short piece of music with which you are very familiar so that you know precisely what any point in the breakdown sounds like in reality.

Synchronisation problems

The piece of music to be broken down should be transferred onto a magnetic track — the crucial consideration here is not whether it is $\frac{1}{4}$ in tape or 8 mm stripe but whether you have the means of transferring that same tape to the finished film in perfect sync. The simplest way is to record the required piece onto a blank piece of striped 8 mm film (preferably clear). If this is a particularly clean recording it can be used later for transferring directly onto your film in frame to frame sync. This can be done by outside companies if you do not have the facility.

If on the other hand you possess a good tape recorder to projecter interlock system then you can keep the $\frac{1}{4}$ in tape as master and use it to transfer the sound onto the final print from, instead of the 8 mm copy which is used for breakdown only. The quality will obviously be better this way. In order to ensure that both the picture and the sound are in sync, it is advisable to use a sync peep about $1\frac{1}{2}$ to 2 seconds before the start of the sound. On the breakdown this peep represents zero and is photographed in the camera as a clear white frame (flash frame). All other frames of both picture and sound are represented by numbers, in sequence, starting with 1, 2, 3, etc. When the flash frame of the picture is placed opposite the peep (in the sound head) the picture and sound will be in sync.

The frame counter

If you photograph a series of numbers from zero to about 500 in

150

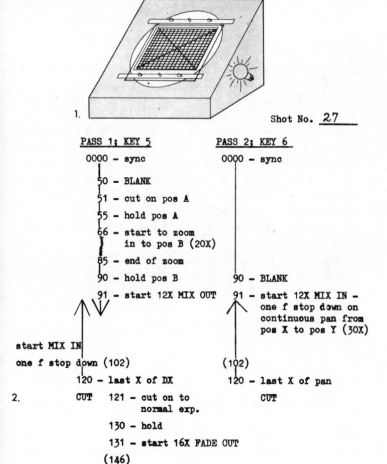

1.

Shot No. 27

PASS 1; KEY 5	PASS 2; KEY 6
0000 – sync	0000 – sync
50 – BLANK	
51 – cut on pos A	
55 – hold pos A	
66 – start to zoom in to pos B (20X)	
85 – end of zoom	
90 – hold pos B	90 – BLANK
91 – start 12X MIX OUT	91 – start 12X MIX IN – one f stop down on continuous pan from pos X to pos Y (30X)

start MIX IN
one f stop down (102)   (102)

120 – last X of DX	120 – last X of pan
2. CUT 121 – cut on to normal exp.	CUT
130 – hold	
131 – start 16X FADE OUT	
(146)	

1, A simple animation table allows you to prepare artwork and shot keys.

2, A dope sheet contains all the information needed to shoot a particular shot.

151

sequence on each frame of a film stock with a magnetic stripe (of course, you can put the stripe on afterwards) you can then transfer the music from your master onto this frame counter. That simplifies the whole process of sound breakdown. You can read out distinctive points in the soundtrack on an editing machine or projector running at slow speed.

However, the best way to do a detailed breakdown is to run your frame counter through the projector at normal speed, with the lens removed. You can reach the film emulsion with a sharp wax pencil. Indicate the beats of the music with a rhythmic movement of the hand. You can pick out various points of specific interest, such as start of phrases or a particular instrument on another run with a different coloured pencil. Put the lens back and run the film again, so that you can check whether your chinagraph marks are in sync. Running the projector at slow speed or even stopping at the marked frames (where this facility is available) enables you to read off the number of the frame. When you have noted down all the main beats, then you can double check it by going through the tune with the aid of the breakdown only. Note down all the additional points that might give you a more complete breakdown with clear indication of what they represent: e.g. trumpets, timpani, violins, start of phrase, etc.

Frame counters and bar sheets

The information from the breakdown of a soundtrack can be in the form of a simple sheet of paper containing a column of numbers running down the page from zero. You note down beats and other components in squares opposite the appropriate number using such symbols as crosses, noughts or asterisks. If the soundtrack being broken down is in fact a composite of several different types of sound, e.g. music, voice, effects ... then each of these is entered in a separate column so that the breakdown of the composite soundtrack can be seen at a glance. The barsheet is used for much longer breakdowns where several separate soundtracks are

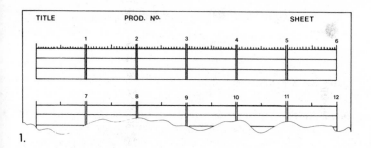

TITLE	PROD. Nº.			SHEET	
FR.	MUSIC	COM.	FR.	MUSIC	COM.
1			51		
2			52		
3			53		
4			54		
5			55		
6			56		
7			57		
8			58		
9			59		
10			60		
11			61		
12			62		
13					

2.

0000 0001 0002 0003 0004 0005 0006 0007 0008 0009

3.

Timing a film needs careful preplanning to achieve the right tempo for each phase. 1, Bar sheet for 18 f.p.s. projection time. You can mark each move and each sound graphically on a simple bar chart. That gives you a fairly visual display of pace.

2, Frame count. A simple frame count tells you just what to do for each frame.

3, A filmed frame counter. Numbering a piece of waste film – or filming a set of numbers produces a counter. You can run that through the projector with the sound track or against a stop watch to calculate your timings.

involved. It runs horizontally and the numbers are divided into bars which can represent either seconds or feet.

Using the breakdowns

Detailed breakdowns of voices are essential for good lip sync and no breakdown can be too detailed in this respect. In the case of music, though, it is very rare that every beat of the breakdown is actually going to represent a cut or a pan. Occasionally it is quite effective to cut on every beat — but this is normally used in quick short bursts where appropriate, otherwise it can become extremely boring.

Nevertheless, it is very important to have as detailed a breakdown as possible to ensure that you really have a complete grasp of the relevant piece of music. Armed with this factual information you can plan your shots knowing exactly how long one particular phrase runs so that you can accommodate a sympathetic camera move which is suggested by it in the time. Of course, the artwork may not sustain such a long pan. In which case it may be better to look for a break in the phrase so that you can use two complementary camera moves; then the detailed breakdown offers an immediate solution. The breakdowns are used in this way not only in planning camera moves but also in getting the animated figures (cartoon and puppet) to move in rhythm with the music.

Camera Effects

Lens attachments

You can fit a variety of attachments in front of the camera lens. Some of them can be fitted in directly (with or without adaptors) and others need special support. A standard filter holder which can be fitted to the front of the lens is very useful but it does not make easy filter changes and the use of gelatine filters is rather restricted. It is well worthwhile making a good filter holder which can accommodate several filter thicknesses. Such a filter holder can be made in the form of a square mount which is attached to a lens hood; standard size filters can be inserted in the opening provided. Unmounted gelatine filters can be used and certain special filters can be prepared and mounted in conventional 35 mm colour slide frames. The square shape also enables your polarising filter to be aligned correctly without any difficulty.

Some cameras are equipped with special holders at the front of the lens designed for holding transparencies and masks for micro-filming. These can be used as ordinary filter holders.

When you are adding a filter holder, make quite sure that the frame does not cause any vignetting or darkening of the image, at any point in the zoom range. 35 mm mounts are easily placed in front of most lenses. If you find that impossible, use $2\frac{1}{4}$ in square mounts instead.

Gauzes

You can make up gauze diffusion filters in 35 mm transparency holders. Mount a piece of thin black gauze material (such as used for making thin scarves) in the transparency holder. The effect of a gauze filter is to soften the focus all over – the exact extent of this depends on the density of the material. It is usually better to have the finest possible material and make up several filters each with a different number of layers to give the desired softening.

Rough artwork where pencil lines are too distinct or the general texture of a painting too rough, can be smoothed out with one layer of gauze. So can rough paintwork on puppets when they are photographed in close-up. Another important application for the gauze filter is in backlight work. Backlit spots of light are made to appear as star shapes – their precise shapes being governed by the type of mesh in the gauze material. The effects are just as good as with much more expensive glass filters, etched or with wire mesh embedded in them.

Other filters

You should mount your neutral density and colour correction filters in the same sizes as they all come in gelatine form and can be easily mounted in slide mounts. The lens polariser is the only exception, because it comes in an integral cine quality glass mount but can be obtained in a variety of sizes.

Masks

Slide mounts can also be used to hold masks of various shapes which are then placed in front of the lens (in the filter holder) as normal filters. In normal photography, the edges of these masks will be out of focus, but with macro focusing facility they can be made to look sharp. Some camera manufacturers supply a selection of masks of shandard shapes, but you can make your own.

It is extremely difficult to attempt to cut a shape out of black paper because of such a small size – the edges are liable to appear rough. A better method is to prepare your masks photographically. Paint or cut out the artwork to a size which is easier to handle. Then photograph it on a 35 mm camera. The result is a mask mounted in a slide holder and ready for use over the lens. Because

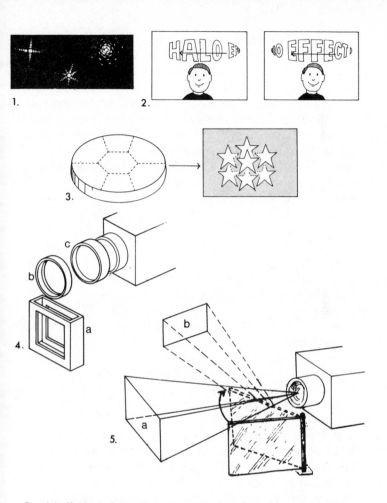

Special effects. 1, Gauze filters can make dots of light appear as stars. 2, Fish-eye attachments can be used to produce a convex effect from flat artwork such as lettering. If the artwork is panned east-west, the lettering appears to move along a halo-like shape. 3, Prismatic lenses can be used to multiply and rotate images. 4, Mounting a filter. Filter holder (a), or filter mount (b), camera lens (c).

5, You can switch from a shooting area in front of the camera (a), to a shooting area at 45% to the camera (b), by means of a pivoting mirror.

of the reduction the edges of a mask produced in this way are very clean and a lot of fine detail can be added to the shape. However, this detail will be lost with normal focusing.

Because of the very nature of this type of masking, the shapes are inevitably black and white, and the density of the black has to be very good to obscure (mask out) the unwanted area. A photographic mask of this kind can be prepared in colour also to give an overall colour to an area of frame instead of masking it off completely. However the result may be a little different from the expected. The colour of the masked off area can only be seen when there is plenty of light in those areas of the scene being photographed and at best it appears as a colour cast over an area of the frame instead of a solid colour which obscures the background. If the colour of a mask were dense enough so that the background scene could not be seen through it, then it would not photograph at all — the result would be the same as with a black and white mask.

Titling masks

Some titling is possible with this method. Inevitably, this means black titles for the same reasons as above. It is important to choose an appropriate background so that the black titles stand out, therefore the lighter the overall scene the better. This is not much of an advantage in flat artwork animation where easier titling methods are available but when shooting puppets or live action it can be extremely useful especially where no rewind is possible for superimposed titles. Of course, the focus range is extremely limited, so most backgrounds will be far out of focus. There is one specific effect which can be obtained this way and which is quite interesting. If the lens is equipped with a macro facility which can be brought into operation following a conventional use of the zoom, then the titles can be brought into focus with it. A pastel coloured title could also be done this way if great care is taken in the line up so that a suitable, clear and unbroken white area forms the background behind the actual lettering.

Split focus close-up lens

Close-up (diopter) lenses have been discussed in an earlier chapter, together with their use for extending the focusing range of a lens in those cameras where the macro-facility is not available. The split-focus diopter lens is much the same as a normal close-up lens in the sense that it brings the focusing of the primary lens forward by a specific amount. However, this is done only over one part of the lens area and the focus over the remainder of the lens area remains unaltered. This way it is possible to combine an extreme close up of some detail and at the same time keep focus at infinity with the use of a standard lens. The split-focus lens should be positioned in such a way that the line of undefined focus between the extreme close up and the infinity lies along a suitable natural line within the picture to make it less noticeable.

Prismatic attachments

Various prismatic attachments are available to create multiple images. The multiplicity depends on the number of facets. When mounted suitably, these prisms can be rotated to produce interesting effects. Another prismatic attachment makes it possible to rotate an image in its entirety around the lens axis and without distortion. This extremely useful device can eliminate the need for a rotation compound on the shooting table. Tilting and rotating the image in this way also expands the scope of puppet animation and can be used equally effectively as a live action effect.

Conversion lenses

Conversion lenses are available for some types of zoom lenses to extend their range at either the wide angle or the telephoto end. They are attached to the front of the zoom lens. These devices sometimes impair the definition slightly. So if you can cover the zoom range you need without one, you are better advised to devise your artwork or setting to suit the main lens.

Kaleidoscope effect

Multiple images and rotation can be produced with a kaleidoscope tube. Ideally the mirrors used should be front silvered. But, since a kaleidoscope is likely to be used only occasionally, you can ignore that aspect.

Mirror effects

There are lens attachments available on the market which enable you to shoot "around the corner", or more precisely at 90° to the lens axis. They clip on at the front of the lens and consist of a mirror set at 45°. This can be very useful for puppet animation where the camera cannot get into a particular spot because of set restrictions. Up shots and down shots are possible this way as well as a rotation through 360°. Naturally, there is a reversal of the image from left to right and this can restrict the application.

Pivoting mirror

A mirror can be mounted in front of the lens in such a way that it can be pivoted around one of its sides which is fixed to the lens mount. Then it can be used to bring a scene into view. It can also serve as a very useful transition aid similar to a wipe by closing on a scene which has been photographed with the mirror at 45° and then opening it out again to reveal a new scene.

A wipe effect becomes possible when two scenes can be set up at 90° to each other; the camera is set facing the main scene and the other scene is set up at 90° to the lens axis so that it can be photographed with the mirror at 45°. To make the operation easier, this scene could simply consist of a photograph. With the mirror at 45° only this scene is visible and the scene in front of the camera is obscured by the mirror itself. The mirror is then pivoted outwards to reveal the scene in front of the camera as the other scene gradually disappears. The mirror edge is not in focus, and so invisible. The impression of a wipe is quite convincing in spite of the inevitable shift of the reflected scene as it disappears.

The camera lens can zoom in and out freely and even the focus can be pulled during the change over to compensate for the possible differences in distances of the two scenes from the camera. It must be remembered that the focus is not on the mirror but on the real object via the mirror, therefore there is no need for a macro-focusing facility. Camera movements are also possible. Great care must be taken to examine or mask off any undesirable light which may be reflected by the mirror. If a two way mirror is used in the same way as described above, double exposures and superimpositions become possible. These are dealt with in greater detail later.

"Snorkel" attachment

To extend your capabilities, you can mount a piece of front-silvered mirror some distance from the lens. For this you might use an extension tube, as used normally for slide copying, but that is not essential. The important thing is that the mirror can be kept at 45° to the lens axis at some distance from the lens. The telephoto end of the zoom is more suited for this purpose because the narrow angle can be covered by a smaller size mirror.

If this attachment is used on a vertical set up (such as is normally intended for flat artwork shooting) then it is possible to take close up side views of solid objects placed on the table, and suitably lit. You can pan along the side of objects such as packets and jars and even go inside them! The objects are moved in the desired direction with the use of table compound movements. If the camera can be moved up and down, or if the mirror itself can be moved toward and away from the lens then it becomes possible to pan up and down as well.

On a normal, three-dimensional set, the camera can be rigged up for aerial shots in this way. It must be remembered though that there is a reversal of geometry of the image because of the use of a mirror – the image is seen upside-down – but the effect is just as interesting. Those few whose cameras have the facility for shooting in reverse will have no problems with this. However the less fortunate ones will simply have to be a little more careful. Remember that this attachment can be rotated at the point where it is fixed to the lens — or at least it can be made to do so. Rotating the mirror through 180° will make the image appear the right way up because the camera is effectively shooting upside down. The rotation of this image is something that should be exploited a great deal for its own sake because it offers exciting possibilities.

There are two ways to overcome the image reversal. You can use a pentaprism — as taken from an SLR camera, or make a periscope. If you can acquire a pentaprism from a discarded SLR viewfinder, just mount it in place of the mirror, flat surface vertical and toward your subject. With the casing and eyepiece removed, you should have a large enough field of view.

A full periscope attachment has no problems because it uses two front-silvered mirrors — one at the bottom and one at the top. The second mirror corrects the geometry reversal caused by the first. Difficult and inaccessible camera angles can be done this way. In solid work, the periscope can get inside the action on the set for close ups and reverse angles, physically impossible any other way.

Capping shutter and cycling

It is quite simple to make up a capping shutter in the form of a blade which can be moved into position over the camera lens. Fix the blade a little way away from the lens on a bracket which allows it to pivot from a position where it is in front of the lens and blocking all the light reaching it, to a position where it is to the side of the lens. The simple red filter holder fitted to many enlargers is a good model of what you want.

With 16 mm, 9.5 mm and Standard-8, the capping shutter can be used for winding the film back and for cycling.

A continually repetitive cycle of drawings or movements (e.g. flames, rocket propulsion, snow etc.) may well consist of only

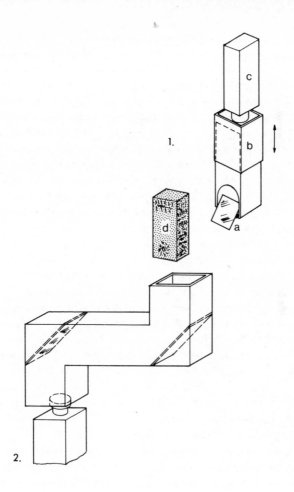

1, A snorkel attachment allows you to film from inaccessable places; (a) mirror (which can be pivoted). (b) Extension tube with facility for adjusting the length. (c) Camera. (d) Three-dimensional object. 2, A periscope is a more sophisticated device producing correctly oriented images, but it is not so convenient to handle.

three drawings. Normally, each one is shot for two frames – one after another and over with continuous changes of artwork. This is very tedious. With a capping shutter (and full windback facilities) you can speed things up. Photograph the first drawing for two frames, then cap the lens for four; open it again for two frames, and so on until you have enough. The artwork remains the same but it is recorded only on those frames where it would fall during conventional shooting; the frames in-between are left unexposed.

At the end of this first run, wind back the film to the start position. Change to the second drawing. Cap the lens for two frames. Then shoot two frames to expose the new artwork in the right place. Continue the two frames on, four frames off sequence over the whole length. Then repeat the process to expose the third set of pairs. You can extend this technique to as many passes (camera runs) as you like, and introduce variation in the number of frames per drawing even within the same cycle – provided you have a reliable frame counter. It is obviously of extreme importance to check the starting position every time because a mistake of only one frame is disastrous. It will run throughout the length of the shot, totally ruining it.

You may want to move the background or some other element during a cycling shot done in this way. You make the move in the normal way – but, of course, you must repeat it *exactly* for each pass. As long as you stick rigidly to the same starting position and make the move the same way, there is no problem. The same applies if there is a pan or zoom during the cycle.

Cycling is particularly useful in those cases where it is difficult to keep the artwork perfectly flat. Even with a good platten you have difficulty with continuous changing of artwork. The platten has to be positioned only once for each pass – therefore a loose piece of glass is sufficient. If it is necessary to pan the background as well, then it is advisable to place a couple of coins at each corner of the loose glass to lift it off slightly (only slightly) so that the background can slide across without moving the platten each time.

Lifting the platten too often is a particular problem with cutout animation because the pieces tend to move very easily. If you are

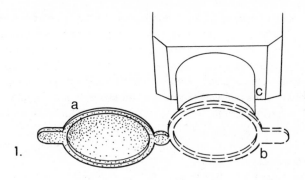

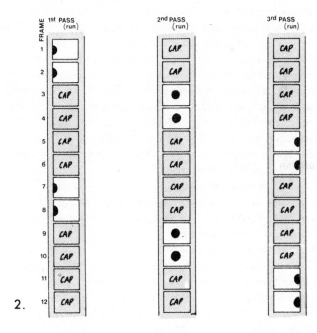

1, You can fit an auxiliary capping shutter without too much trouble; (a) open position, (b) closed position, (c) camera lens.

2, Shooting cycle with a capping shutter speeds up the process considerably.

attempting lip movements – particularly with cutouts, then the use of capping shutter in this way can be of great benefit. Three positions of the mouth: closed; half-open; open, are enough to give a reasonable impression of speech. Each position is shot on a separate pass to a chart which is made up from the careful breakdown of the track of the voice. The shooting has to follow this chart very accurately because the cycling is irregular.

Polariser fades and mixes

The conventional polarising screen has already been discussed. However there is a different application which is worth considering. If two polarisers are placed in front of the lens, and one of them is rotated while the other one remains static, there will be change in the amount of light which passes through to reach the lens. At the point where two axes of polarisation are parallel – most light will pass through; and at the crossed position where the poliarisation axis' of the two are at 90° to each other, very little or no light will pass through. Obviously this can be used to produce fades.

The filters should be mounted in such a way as to eliminate unnecessary play between them, which might alter the relative position of their axes of polarisation. Calibrate the quarter of a circle between the full open and closed positions for more accurate results. You can't just divide the circumference equally, though. Most of the effect is in the last few degrees approaching the fully crossed position. Make a trial exposure with your filters to decide just what calibrations you need. Then you can use the scale for fades and dissolves (see page 62).

Shadow Board Effects

The primary function of a shadow board is to prevent reflection of the camera and its mountings impairing the image of flat artwork. It consists of a matte black board on a frame positioned some distance away from the camera lens and attached to the camera mount (or base). It has a hole just large enough to shoot through. In some cases a "macro frame" is supplied by the camera manufacturer. This can be attached to the camera and used for the same purpose as a shadow board (although it is intended mainly to indicate the point of optimum focus for macro filming when both the background and the artwork mounted on the frame need to appear in sharp focus). For more complicated shadow board effects it is necessary to strengthen this frame.

Artwork placed over the cutout is therefore within the shot. Whether or not it is in focus depends on the lens focus setting, aperture and zoom setting. You manipulate these to the best effect. Most of the effects produced this way are done with normal shooting, although macro-focusing can also be used.

It is also necessary to mask off the light from reaching the front of the artwork on the shadow board in most cases. So it is a good idea to construct the "board" as a box. Make it a simple structure which can be removed easily. For flat artwork shooting, it may be left in position most of the time for its prime purpose – to prevent any scatter from the lights reaching the lens. For puppet work, on the other hand, it is too cumbersome and too limiting to keep in front of the camera all the time.

Shadow board effects apply to both flat artwork animation and puppet work although the precise mechanics of the operation may vary slightly due to the fact that the camera is fixed in a vertical position in one case – and moved freely in a horizontal plane in another. For this reason, the structure of the shadow board needs to be much more solid for puppet work.

Mattes and counter mattes

A matte produced by masking off a section of frame at the shadow board under normal focusing conditions will appear to have a soft edge. The extent of the softness depends on the focal length of the lens, the distance from the lens to shadow board and the position of primary focus.

With macro focusing the mattes become sharp edged. However, you may be very restricted in artwork distance to focus that sharply as well. The key advantage of a soft edged matte is that if used in conjunction with a counter matte the transition between the two images appears less distinct because of the blurred (soft) edges of the mattes. Additionally, any slight misalignment between the matte and the counter matte is less likely to be noticed.

How mattes are used

You can prepare a matte from opaque black paper which is placed over clear glass lying in the aperture of the shadow board. When you have lined up the camera, either by rotoscoping or looking through on to the scene which is to be photographed, place the matte over the glass. Decide its exact position (again by rotoscoping or viewing through) and stick it down firmly — preferably with double sided tape along the edge. If the matte consists of a straight edge which is simply required to cut off a particular area, no special preparations are needed. Just ensure that you have a good straight edge, free of any hairs.

Most commonly, you use a matte and counter matte (or male and female mattes). Each blanks out one part of the scene. The two together would blank it all out. You make your first pass with the first matte in place. So you have now exposed half (say) of each frame with one scene. Wind the film back to your start mark (see page 111). Change to your counter matte, and you are ready to shoot the second half. With your new artwork in place, you now shoot the remainder of each frame.

The simplest way of aligning matte and counter-matte is to leave the matte in place until the counter-matte is stuck down exactly matching it. With the counter matte in place, you can line up the artwork by rotoscoping. Lens iris, focus setting and obviously zoom control must not be altered between the passes.

If the matte is meant to move in some way (perhaps progressively into the shot instead of it being there from the beginning) then you need some form of registration. Start the shot normally without any masking on the shadow board (but the glass remains in position). Put the matte in position exactly when you need it. If extreme accuracy is necessary, check the position by switching all the lights off and rotoscoping. Continue the shot with the section of frame matted out. Wind back the film to the start. Then run it forward, with the shutter capped, to the frame where the matte was introduced. Then make the second pass, with your counter-matte revealing the unexposed position as required.

Split screen effect

By matting out certain sections of the frame and inserting different images in those areas with the help of a counter-matte you have in fact achieved a split-screen effect. The frame can be split into a number of segments with different pictures in each one. The shape of this split can be purely geometric in design, (squares, circles, vignettes) or it can be suggested by the outlines of the shapes being photographed. For example, a shot may end on the close-up of a head in profile. At a given point it is only the outline of the head that remains. Then the picture inside this outline can become something new. It is best to introduce this sort of change with a dissolve unless you particularly want a sudden impact.

You make the necessary mattes for this type of shot by placing a piece of transparent material, such as an acetate cel, over the shadow board glass. Look through the viewfinder with the main artwork in position, and you can trace the outline of the head on the acetate cel with a wax pencil or an audio-visual pencil.

Remove this from the shadow board and stick it to a piece of flat, opaque black paper. Cut out the shape exactly with a sharp scalpel. This gives you male and female mattes in one go.

At the required point in shooting line up the male matte and stick it down. The positioning is very critical in this case and must be checked very carefully. With this matte in place, you continue the pass to record the background. Before the second pass, place the female counter-matte on the shadow board so that it matches the male matte as accurately as possible; and stick it down firmly before removing the male matte. With the counter-matte (female) in position, you can shoot any sort of artwork you want to appear inside the outline of the head.

Movement and shadow board mattes

Perhaps the greatest advantage of shadow-board matting is the freedom of movement of the artwork on the shooting table. Even in the case where the shape of the matte is suggested by the artwork, a considerable amount of movement is possible. You can pan or rotate the table in any direction and change the artwork at will quite independently of the matte which remains in a fixed position relative to the camera and therefore the frame.

The only thing which affects the matte is the zoom, and it is important to keep the focal length at the same setting for both passes through the camera – otherwise the matte and counter-matte will not match. The only possible exception to this is when dealing with vertical and horizontal straight line mattes which go through the centre of frame. The reason for this is that despite the change in the area photographed (or masked off) when the zoom is used at different positions, the relative effects of the mattes is always the same. They always obscure exactly half of the frame along the central line which does not alter its position during the zoom.

The only snag with this is that the softness of the matte edge varies with the change in focal length; and you may produce a more noticeable matte line as a result. Of course, a matte line in

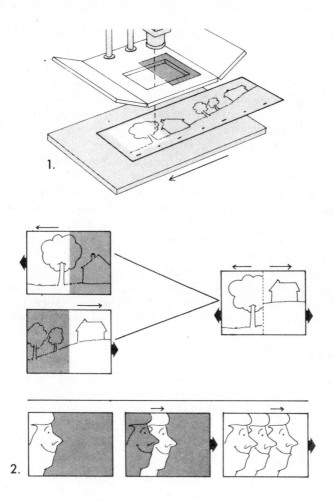

1, Split-screen effects can be done quickly and effectively with a matte and counter matte on the shadow board. The splitting does not have to follow any specific geometric pattern; the outline may be suggested by the shape of the object in the picture. 2, The same image can be multiplied several times, each repeat appearing to move out from behind or out of the first image.

any other position would tend to drift away from the centre towards the edge of frame during a zoom in.

You can still use a zoom movement provided you make the same changes for both passes using male and female mattes in perfect match. Various shaped wipe effects can be produced this way. If the female matte is slightly larger than the frame area when the zoom is at its extreme long focal length end, it will appear to come in from all sides of frame and get smaller as the zoom is moved towards the extreme wide angle position. The interesting thing here is that the female matte shape closes in on a frame area – the same picture that was seen in close-up at the start of the shot is still the only area of the picture to be seen; as it gets progressively smaller with the matte outline it stays the same size in respect to it. The size of the final image depends on the extent of the zoom but it will never disappear. So, you need a dissolve at the end of the zoom to lose it altogether. Alternatively you can make it pop off quite effectively by cutting on fully to the new scene which has been progressively introduced with the use of a male counter-matte on a matching zoom. Tracking (as opposed to zooming) produces a different effect – the outline remains unchanged because so does the focal length.

Filters in place of mattes

Instead of masking out certain areas entirely; it may be useful to simply tint certain areas of the frame a specific colour while leaving others to photograph normally. A version of the above example could then be done with one pass only by making a female matte out of a gelatine filter and placing it over the glass in much the same way as described above. On the zoom out, the area of the artwork surrounding the key interest seen in close-up at the start of the zoom will be visible this time; but it will have an overall colour tint isolating it from the key area of interest, while this area remains the same size in relation to the shape produced by the matte as they both get smaller.

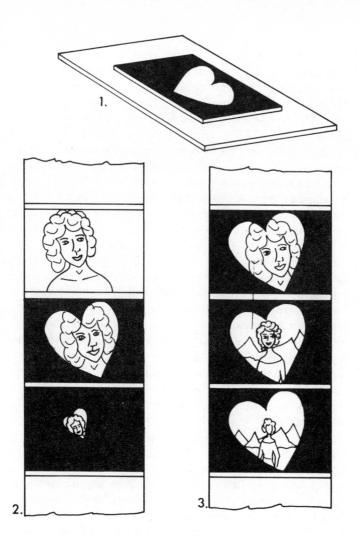

1, Shadow-board masks can be of any shape.

2, Zooming effect on the mask and artwork.

3, Tracking effect on mask and artwork.

Titling

The size of the shadow-board area gives more scope for titling than when this is done immediately in front of the lens. Titles can be handwritten on acetate cels and placed over the glass. It should be possible to accommodate the focusing at wide angles even without a macro facility. The interesting possibilities this offers is to set your title fairly low in the frame so that by zooming in or out on the background scene the title appears to float in and out of the frame. You can enhance the effect by independent panning movement of the artwork on the shooting table. If the focus is not perfectly sharp on the lettering while it is moving in and out of frame, that is quite acceptable as long as it is in focus in the final position.

Additionally, you might pull focus deliberately from the title to the background – particularly at long focal length range of the zoom; a badly out of focus title can then be taken off (or mixed out). But you must replace it with the same type of clear cel to avoid any changes in the exposure.

Naturally these are all black titles. Coloured titles can be used only against large areas of white in the background scene and are not really ideal. The size of the shadow board, though, allows you to do colour titling in one pass. Instead of the conventional black paper, cut the titles out of a piece of opaque coloured paper. On the shadow board, it acts in exactly the same way in obscuring the background scene. Light it from above, and the colour of the paper can be seen. To do this, you must have polarising filters (see page 129). Otherwise the glass will reflect light into the lens. Set the exposure for the bottom scene and light the coloured matte to make it match in (blend in) with it. This is best done by viewing the composite scene through the camera. This kind of effect is enhanced when there is independent movement in the background scene. The self-matting title of this type can be made to move into the frame area gradually – by the use of the zoom, or by being physically moved along the glass – as there is no need to worry about matching counter-matte the movement does not have to be extremely accurate, although that would make it smoother. The main consideration with this approach is focusing, and the size of the frame at the shadow board plane. For the best results, the shadow board should be extended as far as possible from the lens.

Wipes

Conventional wipes are made by progressively obscuring the outgoing scene on the first pass through the camera and then revealing another scene over the same number of frames at the same rate. The wipe outlines can vary in shape and direction of travel across the frame. The most popular ones are in the form of a straight line which moves across the frame (screen) horizontally. If well executed, the wipe appears as a clear line where the outgoing and the incoming scene meet. If mismatching occurs between the two passes this can result in a wobbly line of constantly varying thickness. If the two mattes overlap the line appears black and if they are slightly farther apart the line appears white or overexposed.

Strips of tape can be placed along the edges of the glass on the shadow board and marked with required divisions so that the edges of mattes and counter-mattes can be lined up to them. In practice this is best done just outside the frame area on the shadow board glass so that the two guide points are as close to each other as possible for accuracy.

For greater refinement, you can make up a worm-screw drive to produce wipes of perfect quality. This also enables much finer gradations to be done so that the wipes can take much longer. You can put in a set of registration pegs to register the mattes as well as to actually move them across the frame area. The matte and counter-matte are cut simultaneously from two pieces which are held together in register to ensure a perfect match.

Naturally, wipes done at the shadow board tend to be soft edged, which helps the overall effect. Additionally, the artwork can be moved freely during a wipe in the same way as for any other matting at the shadow board. It is advisable to avoid the use of the zoom during a wipe because the need for a matching zoom tends to produce awkward shots as well as adding one more possibility for creating a mis-match between the matte and the counter-matte.

Static wipe

A static matte on the shadow board which obscures part of the frame can be used to create the effect of a static wipe. The artwork to be revealed, such as a coastline for example, is panned along with the matte line at 90° to the direction of the pan. The matte is positioned so that the artwork appears to be coming out of it – i.e. it is being revealed by the matte line. On the second pass, an identical background (e.g. the blue of the sea area in our example) is photographed through a counter-matte – static. The composite result is that the land appears to materialise from the sea.

This can be used in conjunction with a conventional wipe which stops short as it wipes across the screen. The movement carrying on the effect is continued in this way. Various images can appear over plain background. For the best effect, only a small area should be masked off and the background should occupy a fairly noticeable area and not be completely obstructed by the main image.

Ripple glass effects

Various types of glass can be placed in the aperture of the shadow board to distort the image. This does not have to be special glass, but the type which is available for various domestic and industrial uses with patterns of varying sizes and with varying distortion properties. Pay special attention to the focusing. It may have to be altered from the normal setting. However, as the best transition to and from a ripple glass effect is through a dissolve, the change in focus is not likely to be noticeable. Glasses which appear to be only slightly distorted are usually the most effective because the image can be seen to resemble its original form without a drastic change.

The real effect comes from moving the glass slightly in between each frame during the shooting. This should be done in a specific direction and at a constant speed to produce a nice rippling effect. A worm-screw device such as that mentioned earlier for use with wipes can be a great help. Circular movements of the glass are also very effective. Experiment with different glasses while looking through the camera in order to choose the most suitable one for a particular purpose. You may have to place the glass a long way from the camera lens to achieve good focus. If the shadow board does not extend that far, another type of support may need to be used. The further you move the glass from the lens, the finer the ripple, there are more distortion points covered by the lens. In the case of backlit artwork, such as lettering for example, the best results are achieved by placing the ripple glass directly onto the artwork.

Table Top Effects

Matting at the table top level produces sharp edge mattes because the matte edge lies exactly in the cameras focus plane. Focus away from the matte, and the artwork goes unsharp. Sharp edged mattes are useful where a clearly defined edge is required. When counter-mattes are used, hard-edged mattes require a greater degree of accuracy than do soft-edged ones. On the other hand, tracing out an accurate shape for the matte to fit specific contours and outlines with the artwork is much more easily done at the table top level than on the shadow board and should be used to full advantage.

Split screen

Split screening is done in the same way as with the shadow board mattes, except that there is severe restriction on the artwork below the matte. Vertical and horizontal movements and certain other diagonal movements can be done only if a straight edged matte is used and it lies parallel to the direction of the pan. Alternatively the artwork can be panned on a moving peg-bar while the matte is registered to a second pegbar which can be of either fixed or moving type. Zooming is only possible when a straight matte line passes through the horizontal or the vertical centre of the frame and is therefore not subject to drifts. Matte lines running from one corner of the frame to the other will also escape the drift but they are much more difficult to determine in practice than the horizontal and vertical. This applies naturally to the type of split-screening where different elements entirely unrelated in size and with different and opposing movements are assembled together in one composite frame. If the artwork is carefully prepared so that the same field sizes and the same camera moves can be used for all relevant passes, a variety of split-screening shots are possible.

Image break up

The key to matting at table top level is that the matte moves with the artwork whenever the table compound is moved (although a certain amount of movement is possible on the pegbars alone). This restriction can in fact be turned to good use and become a positive advantage. For example, the image can be made to break up along certain lines and then all the different elements move apart until the frame is left completely blank. The break up lines can follow a purely geometric shape unrelated to the picture within the frame or they can be suggested by the outlines of the picture content. In either case, the outlines of the break up are traced out on a sheet of punched transparent paper or cell in register with the artwork. You then use this tracing to cut suitable mattes out of black paper.

The ideal paper for this purpose is thin *glossy black* – because under polarised lighting it does not photograph at all. The number of mattes required, of course, depends on the number of segments that the frame is being divided into. Each mask should cover all but one segment. Cut them all simultaneously, even if this means that some of the cuts will have to be made good again. You can "mend" mattes with thin tape on the reverse side of the paper. Identify each segment clearly to avoid getting into a muddle.

Plot out a movement for each segment with the appropriate matte in position over the artwork to find out the precise point at which that segment will be out of frame. If you are zooming in as well as panning, this reduces the actual distance the segments have to be panned to the side and makes them appear to fly towards the camera as they break up. The angle of this drift towards the camera is determined by the extent of the zoom. Smaller ratio zooms will make the segments move towards the camera slightly as they drift out of frame but larger ratio zooms will make them come towards the camera at a much sharper angle before they disappear out of frame.

When you have made all the preparations, shoot the scene up to the zero point – the frame before the start of the break up. Check the zero position of the table at this time if any other moves have been involved up to this point. Place the first mask on the artwork and carry out the appropriate movement. Each subsequent segment is shot on a separate pass through the camera starting at zero position both in the camera and the table set up.

Wipes

Hard edged wipes can be done at the table top with the aid of the pegbars. In many ways this is the easiest way of doing wipes because you already need some form of moving pegbar system, even with the simplest set ups. Because of the sharp edge you must have the highest possible accuracy. Naturally there is a limitation on the movement of the artwork (unless you have a secondary moving pegbar) and the field sizes of the two scenes to be joined with a wipe have to be identical, as in the case of the shadow board wipes. Additionally the table must also remain in the same position for both the wipe-out and the wipe-in pass. This requires careful planning to ensure that the artwork is pegged correctly so that the appropriate areas of the artwork are covered on both passes at the same table set up. If any additional moves are required after the wipe, try them out and note down the relevant position before you begin shooting, because it is not advisable to move the table once the wipe out has been shot.

Animated wipes

The larger area of the table top lets you prepare a different type of wipe relatively easily. Instead of the wipe line remaining constant throughout the wipe — regardless of its shape — you can make it flexible. It can take on shapes during the wipe or it can start as a distinct shape which then becomes fluid and finally disappears out of the frame as the new scene is introduced. You can use the shape of an animated object in the incoming scene as the shape of

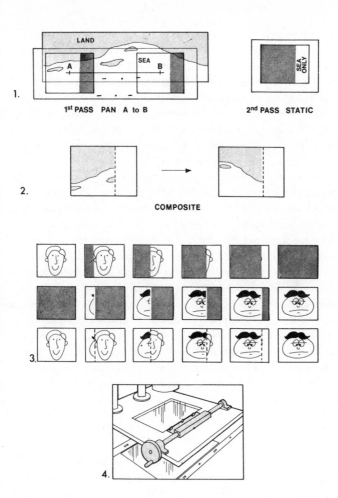

Wipes with fixed matte. 1, With the shadow board matte fixed, the sea shore artwork is panned. Then with the counter-matte, sea only is printed into the space. 2, So the land appears to materialise from the sea as the pan continues.

3, Conventional soft-edged wipes can be executed with moving mattes on the shadow board. 4, The mattes can be moved on a pegbar attached to a worm-screw drive on the shadow board.

the wipe matching the movements of the same figure until the point of final reveal.

The mattes and counter-mattes are prepared in much the same way as other animation artwork. Sketch out a general guide of the progressively changing shape first, taking into account the length of the wipe in time (i.e. the number of frames). As in normal animation, you can shoot each cell (or in this case matte) on two frames or more – provided exactly the same shooting pattern is followed for both wipe-out and wipe-in passes.

Shoot the outgoing scene normally up to the point where the wipe should start. Place the first of the series of wipe-out mattes over the artwork just as you would an animation cel. Photograph it and each succeeding matte according to the dope sheet. When you have completed the wipe-out pass, wind back the film so that a new scene can be revealed with the use of the matching series of counter-mattes. Incidentally, you should cut each pair of mattes and counter-mattes out of the same piece of paper.

Alternatively, you can wipe to black first and then reveal the next scene from black. This way no rewinding is necessary. The wipe-out is shot in the same way as above followed by the wipe-in with the counter-mattes. Obviously the mattes and counter-mattes do not have to be a perfect match. Another alternative is to use only one set of mattes – wiping from black in the reverse order.

Push-off wipes

The fact that the matte moves with the artwork in the case of table top wipes can be used to create a push-off effect. A scene is progressively pushed out of frame by the incoming one. The push can be in any direction.

You can do a push-off wipe at the end of a shot involving many complicated camera moves. But it is most easily explained as a transition between two static shots. Place the matte just outside the edge of frame on the opposite side to the direction of travel. As the table is panned progressively in this direction, the picture is moved out of frame and replaced by black paper. With the table at

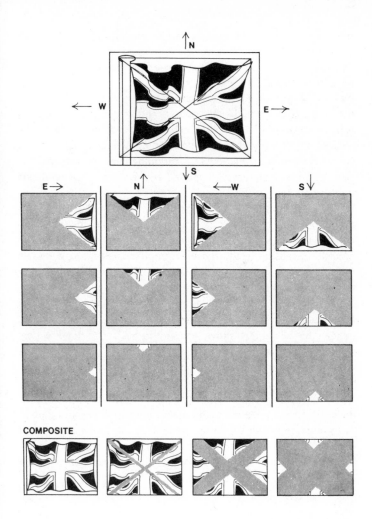

COMPOSITE

Image break-up. A guide is made first to determine the shape. Each segment is shot on a separate pass through the camera while the others are masked off. By careful application of zoom and rotation, the segments can be made to spin or float in depth.

the start position again (and the film wound back), put the artwork of the new scene into position. Substitute the matte with its counter-matte which completely covers the frame, extending just beyond the edge.

As you repeat the pan, the new scene is progressively brought into the frame while the black counter-matte protects the already exposed areas of frame. On projection the first scene appears to be pushed out of frame by the incoming one. At the end of the wipe the counter-matte is just outside the frame line – on the opposite side. It can now be removed altogether and the shot can continue unobstructed.

When preparing the artwork for push-off wipes, the key considera- tion of the identical field sizes and identical set up of the table app- ly just as with the others. However, where there is a great deal of precision available in the movements of the table top, a certain amount of adjustment is possible with straight edged vertical or horizontal mattes. This adjustment can be done only in the same direction in which the matte line runs – and not in the direction the matte itself moves. If the new artwork is pegged to a secondary pegbar this will enable the adjustment in the horizontal direction. However it is best to plan out the push off wipe and peg the artwork in such a way that no other adjustments will be necessary. Without the wind-black facility a kind of "push-off" wipe is possi- ble where the outgoing picture is pushed out by a mask which in turn is replaced by the new scene coming into frame at the same rate of pan and in the same direction. This can be made much more interesting by using a coloured paper as a mask (instead of black). Also, the incoming artwork can come from a different direction.

Push-off wipes in puppet animation

In the case of solid set ups, the wipes are done mainly on the shadow board. Push-off wipes are perhaps the only ones that can be done successfully at the set level. Unlike flat-artwork wipes, of course, you move the camera instead of the artwork. To make

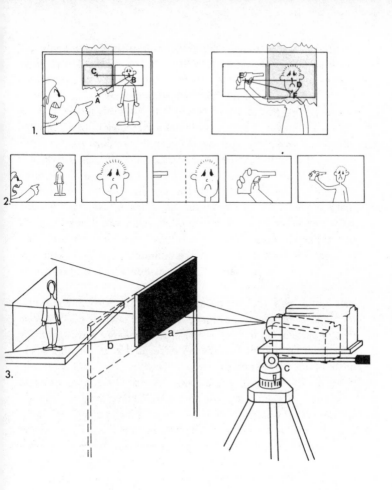

The push-off wipe. 1, Shot key showing first and second phases, with mattes. 2, Effect of shot.

3, With solid sets, you can achieve a push-off effect by panning the camera from the scene to a black mask (a). Move the mask (b), return the camera to its start position (c), rewind the film, and you can now pan again so that your (new) scene "pushes off" the old one.

things easier, you may decide to zoom in from a wide angle to a close-up or medium shot before the wipe is to start. At this point, place a matte between the camera and the scene – or even on the set itself, if you are using polarised lighting. It should be on a firm, solid support. If it is placed on an independent support at some distance from the scene, there is the added benefit of a soft edge which can overcome any inaccuracies in the pan. On the other hand, a sharp edge can be quite effective. If a mismatch is likely to occur it is better to have a black line (or even a wider strip) between the two pictures than an overlap. In any case, with the matte just outside the edge of frame pan (or tilt) the camera to the point where the scene is completely blacked out. Mark the point on the pan (or tilt) scale, and divide the distance into segments (increments) to indicate the desired amount of movement per frame. Make the move as planned. Then redress or alter the set as required for the wipe in.

Pan the camera back to the start position so that you can put in the counter-matte. At the start position, the counter-matte covers the frame fully, so that when the pan is repeated it will gradually reveal the new scene. In fact the effect is that of the new scene pushing out the first one.

It is important to give due consideration to the change of angle which occurs during a push off wipe. When the wipe-in is accomplished, the camera will in fact be pointing in a different direction than at the start of shot. This difference obviously depends on the amount the camera needs to be panned, which in turn depends on the picture area covered by the lens, i.e. a close up at the telephoto end of the zoom will require less panning than a wide shot.

If the matte is independently supported, then the entire set can be moved, shifted or even substituted if necessary. The line up can be checked with the counter-matte in position, but without altering anything else on the camera set up. Any other movements can be anticipated and improvised during the shooting after the wipe operation has been completed.

There is one other sort of wipe that you can do on a solid model set. You can move up (or zoom in) onto a character or object until it fills the screen. For example, you might zoom in on a truck travelling along a city street, once the truck fills the frame, you alter the whole set to a country lane; zoom out again, and your scene has changed.

Double Exposure
and Superimpositions

As we have already seen, dissolves, split-screening and wipes require more than one exposure to be made on the same piece of film. Most of these techniques involve masking off certain frame areas so that each new exposure is made in an area of frame which has been previously unexposed. Double exposure, however, requires a double run of film through the camera but no masking of any kind. A dissolve is, of course, a double exposure effect; but whereas the dissolve involves a continual change of emphasis between the two overlapping scenes, the double exposure is constant. It is the same as picking one frame during a dissolve and "freezing" it.

Exposing the double exposure

If the two scenes to be superimposed over each other were both of the same density and the double exposure were done simply by exposing one scene first at normal exposure and then the second one over it also at normal exposure – the results would of course be an overexposed picture. This is because the film emulsion is receiving double the light (200%) when it is exposed twice at full normal exposure. When you make two or more exposures on each frame, the *total* exposure must add up to a single normal exposure (100%).

If you want two scenes to be of equal density, then each one has to be underexposed by the equivalent amount so that the film emulsion receives the equivalent of full normal exposure. In practice this means that both scenes should be underexposed by one *f* stop (50% of normal).

When the double exposure does not start at the beginning of a shot but some way in, the shot is exposed normally up to that point (at full exposure). From then, the iris is stopped down by one *f* stop or a 0.3 N.D. filter is placed over the camera lens. The second scene is then exposed over this section of the film also at one *f* stop below the normal exposure. If the previous scene has cut out at a certain point, then the exposure on the second scene is compensated by opening the iris one *f* stop at that point (or taking out the N.D. filter) and continuing the shot at normal exposure.

Balance ratio

It is not always necessary to maintain a 50–50 ratio between the two scenes. If a scene is required to predominate then it can be given 60 or 70 per cent of the full exposure. In fact the balance between the two scenes can be varied at will during the double exposure. This of course applies to the type of scene where the picture is evenly exposed over the whole frame area and the overall scene has a full range of tones.

Occasionally there may be large dark areas within the frame composition. If an image on a dark background is to be superimposed in this area only, then the exposure guides mentioned above do not apply. The dark area is already underexposed and a 50–50 exposure ratio would give the composite image a correct balance between the two elements but an overall exposure of the film would be down by 50%. Therefore in this case both elements should be photographed at normal full exposure. A composite picture of this kind resembles a matted shot more than a superimposition, because of the very absence of the overlap between the two scenes. If you wish to insert something into a live scene with the appropriate dark area, this is the best way. Either the animated or the live element can be shot first and at different times — provided you make a careful note of sync point and a sketch of the area where the added image will be inserted. This should be done in relationship to the real or imaginary guide lines in the viewfinder. That way, a live action character can be inserted into a suitable animation scene (either puppet or flat).

Unsuitable scenes

If a scene contains a great amount of white areas it is not likely to work well in a superimposition. Pure white "burns out" the film emulsion because it is on the limit of the tonal range that can be registered. Areas of average density in the second scene will not register at all over this area unless the exposure ratio favours the second scene very substantially. This in turn results in the darker areas of the first scene failing to register at all.

Dissolves and double exposure

The double exposure is most effective when it appears in an otherwise ordinary shot. It can be introduced and lost by means of a straight cut and very often this suits the action best. On the other hand the double exposure can be made to appear very gradually. At the start of the double exposure, you do a normal dissolve-out (to black). Wind back the film to the start and execute a dissolve-in of the same length over exactly the same scene, only this time you alter the exposure by one *f* stop, either on the iris or with the N.D. filter. The result (at this stage) is thus a dissolve from full to half exposure. Of course, if there has been any action during the dissolve out, it has to be repeated on the dissolve in over the same frames. Otherwise you can choose a suitable static moment to perform the transition. Shoot the rest of the scene at this same exposure and if the superimposed scene is to be lost again at a certain point leaving the first scene on its own, then the operation is performed again. After a dissolve out, the same picture is dissolved in again but this time the exposure is opened up to normal. On the second pass (the third for the dissolved sections) through the camera, the superimposed scene is dissolved in at the same point and over same frames as on the first pass – and the exposure used is one *f* stop below normal.

Without dissolve facility

If you do not have an automatic rewind to the start of the dissolve and the film has to be rewound manually each time then this may prove to be a very laborious task indeed. The cuts in and out of double exposure can be softened with a certain amount of manipulation of the lens iris even without the use of dissolves. It must be remembered that this method only softens the cuts and the results are not the same as a true dissolve. Divide up the ring on the lens iris into as many fine increments as possible between the stop representing the normal exposure and one stop below it. At the point where the double exposure is to be introduced stop down the lens iris progressively from the standard exposure f stop to one stop less. This transition can be extended by shooting on two or more frames per increment.

Once you reach the double exposure setting, shoot the scene at this stop as long as required. On the second pass, perform the operation in reverse. Start at the beginning of the double exposure with the second artwork, and the lens set *two* stops below normal. Open up the lens iris progressively to the double exposure stop. With the use of N.D. filters you can use the same f stop as for the first pass and therefore the same scale.

Double exposure with a two-way mirror

A two-way mirror which partially transmits and partially reflects the light can be placed at 45° in front of the camera lens so that two scenes can be shot simultaneously. The lighting of the two scenes should be matched so that under normal conditions they would both be shot at the same f stop. Generally speaking, the transmission to reflection ratio of a two way mirror is around 60:40 rather than precisely 50:50. However this difference of 1/3 of an f stop is not worth worrying about at this stage and to all practical purposes we can calculate with a ratio of 50:50. It is just as important with this type of double exposure or super imposition to expose the film emulsion correctly as when it is done in two separate passes. But as the mirror "absorbs" the light in roughly equal proportions from both scenes — and this is roughly equivalent to one f stop, with most mirrors of this type the actual f stop for a double exposure remains the same as that for individual exposure of each scene.

Restrictions and advantages

The main drawback of this type of double-exposure is that both scenes have to be photographed simultaneously which makes it only really suitable for horizontal set ups. The advantage, of course, is that you see a composite superimposed scene through the viewfinder and you can check the correct balance ratio between the two elements and adjust it as required. It is possible in fact, to light certain areas within the two scenes so that they blend in or stand out more.

You can introduce such a double exposure into a normal scene, but the procedure is somewhat different. It is best to line up both scenes first and establish the correct lighting balance. Black out one of the scenes with clean black velvet draped a little way beyond the mirror. The exposure must now be compensated by opening up the iris one f stop (where 50:50 ratio is used). At the point where the double exposure should start, set the exposure back to normal and remove the black velvet to reveal the second scene.

If the double exposure is to be introduced with a dissolve the operation is similar to that described earlier. At the point where the double exposure is to be introduced, make a dissolve out. Follow that by a dissolve in (over the same frames) with the masking removed and both scenes visible, and the appropriate adjustment to the exposure.

Movement in the double exposure

Double exposure is most effective when there is not only a marked difference in the two superimposed scenes, but a fair amount of movement as well. This can be either a movement within the frame, camera movement only, or ideally a combination of both. When it is done using two passes through the camera there are no

192

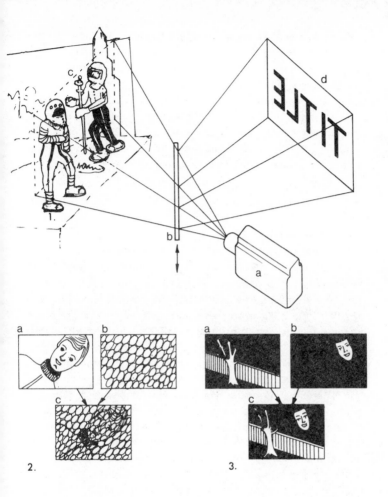

1, Double exposure with a two-way mirror. (a) Camera. (b) Two-way mirror. (c, d) Scenes to be overlayed. If the mirror is moved out from the start of the shot, it can be used to "wipe-in" scene d over scene c as it is moved gradually back into position.

Double exposure. 2, Scenes (a) and (b) are photographed on the same piece of film at a 50:50 ratio. 3, Because of the large black areas in scenes (a) and (b) they can be photographed on the same piece of film without exposure compensation.

movement restrictions of any kind; but this is not the case with the use of a two-way mirror. Any camera movement during the double exposure affects both scenes. This can be exploited deliberately to create a strange unison in the movement — as though absolutely identical camera moves have been made on two separate passes. This is particularly enhanced if the scenes are given a certain amount of conventional movement by tracking or rotating the entire little set. The camera should be mounted with the front of the lens at the pivoting point as discussed earlier.

Wiping-in a double exposure

If the mirror mount is made so that the mirror can slide in and out, it is possible to use this to create the effect of the double exposure being introduced in the form of a wipe. The mirror is pulled back so that the scene in front of the camera can be photographed directly at normal exposure. At a given point, the mirror is moved forward into its normal position progressively introducing the second scene as a superimposition. It is important that the leading edge of the mirror is left clear when the mirror is mounted into a frame. The exposure remains the same throughout this operation. Naturally, a wipe-out of the superimposed image is possible when the operation is performed in reverse. However, when the scene to be wiped out is in fact the first scene which was shot with the camera looking at it directly another approach has to be used. This involves a second mirror, front silvered and fully reflecting, which is moved in gradually in front and parallel to the two-way mirror. This way the scene in front of the camera is progressively obscured as the light from the second scene (at 90° to the lens axis) is directed fully towards the camera lens. The exposure remains unaltered for this operation also.

Superimposed titles — white lettering

The technique involved in superimposing titles over a scene is much the same as already described for double exposures with one vital difference: there is no exposure compensation between passes. If you have backwind facilities, use the normal two-pass system of superimposition unless the use of the mirror contributes to the creation of a specific effect. The normal method offers a lot more scope.

The two separate exposures can be made at different times and in different locations. A title can even be shot before the background scene and the background scene can be anything either live or animated with any kind of camera movement imaginable. The only consideration is that you should frame the picture to avoid bright or very light subjects from appearing in the titling area. This means that you can photograph the main title of your holiday movie at home before you go (including fade-in and fade-out). Rewind the film to the head and shoot the title background on that cartridge when the occasion arises. As with any exposed film, of course, there should not be a great gap in time between the first exposure of the film and processing. Of course, movements are totally independent of the background; and, perhaps more important, so is focus. You can alter the sharpness of background and titles independently.

The background for the titles should ideally be in the range of dark to middle grey in black and white terms. Bright pastel coloured backgrounds do not give enough contrast to the white lettering to make it stand out. With borderline cases it is advisable to open up the iris a little and help the lettering to burn in fully. Alternatively, the background scene can be slightly underexposed.

If you use the two-way mirror approach to titling, you most compensate for the loss of light through the mirror on the background scene by opening the lens iris one f stop. Illuminate the black and white title with the same amount of incident light as the background scene, and make no allowance for the high reflectivity of the white lettering. It is this high reflectivity which enables the white lettering to burn in onto the film emulsion so that the background scene at those points is destroyed. The only reason for using the two-way mirror approach for superimposed titles is when there are no means for rewinding the film for a second exposure or when a specific effect is required.

Moving titles

When you superimpose the titles on a second pass through the camera they can be moved, distorted and generally messed around with to produce some interesting effects. The primary requisite here is that during the exposure of the title, nothing else but that title is recorded on the film. This is achieved by preparing the artwork on glossy black paper or card (or even glossy black photographic paper) and shooting with polarised lighting. Alternatively the titles can be prepared photographically on a lith type film, such as Kodalith, and lit from behind (backlit). Kodalith is a lithographic film of very high contrast which can be used in much the same way as ordinary photographic paper.

Backlit lettering of this type is ideal because no matter how much the letters may be overexposed deliberately the background will not photograph — provided all the light is behind the artwork and there is no spill-light. This means that theoretically you can make an indefinite number of passes through the camera. Additionally, the letters can be made to flow or pulsate by opening up the lens iris gradually and overexposing them deliberately. In the case of top-lit lettering this is not possible to the same extent even with the strongest polarising filters. However, multiple exposure with polarised toplit lettering are generally just as good at normal exposures. You can move the titles on the animation table, or make them appear to move with various camera movements.

It is not necessarily the entire title which has to move as a whole; each letter can be isolated and moved around tracing an individual path of its own. If each letter is moved in this way on a separate pass, but over the same section of film, then the title can appear to come together out of a number of unconnected letters floating around in the frame. Trace a path for each letter on the pantograph table. There is no need for very great accuracy — except at the point where all the letters join up to form a word. Don't shoot this zero point with each letter on a separate pass. End the separate passes on the frame before the zero point and when you have done them all, reveal the entire title and photograph it as a complete word during the hold starting with the frame which would normally be the last frame of movement for each letter. The reason for this is that any inaccuracy in the registration would show up more when the lettering is in one static line then when each letter is moving independently through the frame.

The zoom is a great aid in this type of work because it enables the letters to be moved in depth so that some can be coming nearer the camera while others are moving away into the distance at the same time. You can make the complete title fly into position from outside the frame with the use of the zoom alone if it is positioned at a suitable point away from the centre of frame so that the drift produced by the zoom appears to bring the lettering into the frame or move it out. This movement in depth is most effective when superimposed over a static or slow panning scene. Avoid it, though, over zooms in the background picture unless the zooms are accurately synchronised to coincide with each other and move in opposite directions.

Superimposing colour titles

You can superimpose coloured titles only over dark, unexposed or underexposed areas of frame. The reason for this is that they cannot be burnt in like the white titles. If you increase the exposure on a coloured title to make it burn in – it will then reproduce as white and the whole point of the exercise is lost.

Pastel colours are most suitable, because they stand out better against a dark background than say deep red or blue. Ideally the background should not only be dark but have as little colour as possible. When colour is mixed on a film emulsion the result is the same as when the paints of the equivalent colours are mixed on a palette, i.e. they produce an intermediary colour. So a green title on a red background will reproduce as yellow. The colour of the title will in fact appear different at every point where it mixes with a distinct colour in the background and the result can be very disappointing. You can prepare coloured titles in the same way as white, then colour them with a filter in front of the lens. Correct colour reproduction depends very much on the exposure. If, for example, you want your title to be a dark red it is no use giving it a little more exposure to make it register better — all this will do is to produce a much lighter red.

Ripple glass and focus pull

You can add virtually any camera effect to your superimposed titles: fade them at a specific point over a scene; with the aid of a mask make them appear through an invisible line in the frame; shoot through ripple glasses to make them change shape; prepare them as animation cells with ever changing shapes; or use suitable camera movements (on their own or with other effects) to achieve greater range of movement.

Ripple glass distortions can be introduced through dissolves to produce much smoother effects. Fades and dissolves are also very effective when used in conjunction with focus pulls. You can start the fade-in with the title lettering completely out of focus and, during the fade, pull the focus gradually to the normal sharp position. The effect produced this way is of the lettering materialising out of a faint mist which is slowly clearing up. An out of focus image of the title can be faded up in a small area of screen or popped on in sync with the music; a quick zoom in and a simultaneous focus pull can transform this indefinite patch of mist into a bold title in close-up. The scope is unlimited from the simple reveal to the dramatic breaking up of the lettering.

Flop-over box

A flop-over box is a simple but effective device which is easy to make and can be used on both horizontal or vertical set ups. Mount a piece of clear glass in a wooden frame which fits into a rectangular box in such a way that it can be pivoted. You will need either grooves in the frame and nails protruding from the box, or vice versa. Fit velvet to the edges of the frame so that no light can get between it and the box as you pivot the frame. The main

1.

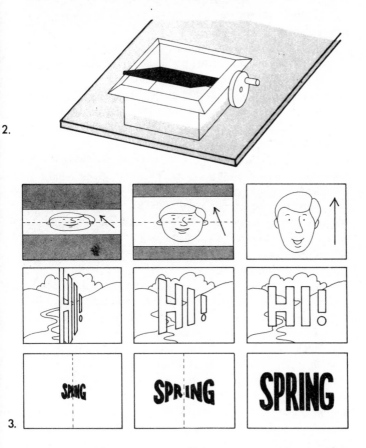

2.

3.

1, With multiple shooting, you can move independently each element of your scene (against a black background).

2, With a flop-box, you can produce a variety of moving effects on the table top, 3.

pivoting points are along the vertical and the horizontal centre lines of the glass frame. These are normally lined up to the vertical or horizontal lines of the picture frame; but pivoting the glass frame at the corners can be just as effective. As with any other movement, you need to use measured increments. So, you must incorporate a pointer on your flop-over box to read against a suitable scale.

Prepare lettering on a lith film. Stick that down to the glass. The lighting is from behind the artwork so you must take care to mask out all areas. As you rotate the glass and frame from a position parallel to the lens axis, to one perpendicular to it, the lettering appears to materialise from a central line.

You can mask off the lettering along the pivoting line and shoot on two passes through the camera to achieve a symmetrical effect on both sides of the screen. Make the moves on each pass in the opposite directions. You can add to the effect by zooming at the same time.

The flop-over box is not used only for giving movement to superimposed titles but can also be used to flop-over an image which may be covering the screen fully. This effect can be a useful alternative to a conventional wipe or fade out — and it does not require windback.

You need a reasonably large transparency of each piece of artwork. At the end of a scene, substitute the transparency on the flop-box *exactly in register* for the artwork. When the image has been flopped over to the disappearing point, substitute the transparency, and reverse the operation. If you put the new artwork on the opposite side of the glass, the rotation can be continued in the same direction. In this case you will have to adjust the masking at the disappearing point to enable the frame to pivot through a complete circle.

More mirror effects

Image break up can be done with the use of a piece of front-silvered mirror to act as a transition from one scene to another.

This operation is quite simple – the mirror is actually broken. You need a thin mirror so that when pressure is applied on the edges it will crack fairly easily. Line up the camera and shoot directly at what is to be the second or the incoming scene. Stage the first, out-going, scene at 45° to the camera axis so that it can be seen via the front silvered mirror. Of course this sort of transition can only be done with static set ups in both scenes. What's more you must shoot continuously instead of single frame and that at the highest available speed. The slow motion effect of shooting at high speed slows down the shattering process and the results can be quite – shattering!

You can, alternatively, make the image break up with this set up by scratching the surface off the front silvered mirror progressively. Where the mirror surface has been removed, there is clear glass through which the scene in front of the camera is photographed. As random patterns are scratched on the mirror, less and less remains of the original scene, until it is completely replaced by the new scene. Yet another alternative is to scrach out a shape on the front silvered mirror – or even lettering for a title. The fill-in area does not have to be a full scene but simply clearly diffused light, with perhaps a coloured filter in front of it, or some kind of coloured pattern (such as a moiré pattern or a filter mosaic, which can be made up by sticking together small random shapes of coloured gelatine).

The fill-in area can be either inside the lettering or outside it, in the same way as the shape can be made out of the clear areas in the glass or the mirrored surfaces. In all these cases the exposure is normal as if the scene were being shot directly, because the scratching process is self-matting. A two way mirror can also be used in a variety of ways. If it is shattered as described above it can be a very dramatic exit from a double exposure.

Inserting live action

A lot of the techniques discussed earlier can be used to combine certain types of live action with puppet or flat artwork animation. If you can position mattes and counter mattes easily and accurately on a shadow board (which, if portable, is the equivalent of an effects box), then you can attempt a lot of composite shots involving live action elements. It is imperative that the mattes be kept in constant relationship to the camera lens for the two separate exposures. The matte lines should follow any available shapes within the frame, so that the transition point between the live action segment and the animated one is less noticeable. Take particular care to match the lighting conditions, with emphasis on the shadows. In fact a deliberate use of shadows can hide the matte line very effectively.

Mirror matting

The technique involving scratching off the surface from a front silvered mirror can be used to enable the shooting of a live action insert into a puppet set or a painted background. Photograph the set via a front silvered mirror at 45° to the lens axis as usual. As we have seen earlier with the use of a nodal point head, you can pan and zoom to create an even greater illusion.

Suppose that one of the windows in our set building will be used to insert a live figure pulling up the blind and looking out. Trace the outlines of this window carefully on to the mirror; this operation is done by looking through the camera. Scrape off the mirror surface from this area so that the set window is no longer visible. Set up a real blind at an appropriate distance in front of the camera – the outline of the blind can be used to help with the line up. When you light this area to match the model set the two blinds to achieve composite effect. The main obstacle is the lack of depth of field because the live subject is inevitably a lot farther away from the model set. So, make sure your ideas will work before you start building.

Mirrors on the set

It is possible to shoot very high or very low angles by placing a

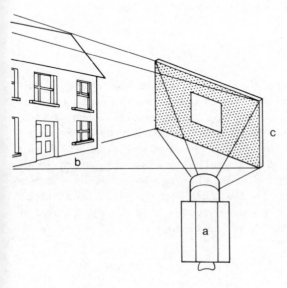

You can incorporate live inserts with a suitably arranged mirror. (a) Camera. (b) Model building. (c) Front silvered mirror with window section left clear (surface scratched off). (d) Live action set.

mirror in the appropriate position on the set. For example, you can make an up-shot of a puppet on a balcony by placing a mirror on the floor of the set at a suitable angle; shoot down directly from above, with the camera upside-down to compensate for the geometry reversal of the image. To get round an awkward camera move, you can mount a mirror over the set so that it can be pivoted in the middle. Then you don't have to move the camera to change the angle. You just pivot the mirror gradually.

Old favourite

There is of course the old favourite mirror shot of indefinite multiplication of images. Two mirrors are used on opposite sides to each other and with the subject in between. The camera looks over the top of one of the mirrors onto the subject and its many reflections in the mirror behind it. By panning (or better still, by dollying the camera along the edge of the mirror) you can gradually change the angle at which the line of multiple images lie to the camera axis. Alternatively, the mirror nearest the camera can be progressively obscured or revealed ... it can also be tilted or twisted to produce additional distortions.

The Projected Image

You can photograph a transparency directly on an animation table with the use of backlight. But it must be of a reasonable size if any movement such as zooming or panning is to be incorporated. Straightforward copying is not very difficult particularly with the aid of macro facilities but that is more-or-less the limit.

The effective size of a transparency can be increased by projecting it and photographing the projected image instead. You need a suitable screen in place of the backlight glass. There are a variety of materials that can be used for this from specially produced back projection screens to ordinary ground glass. Opal glass (milky acrylic plastic) is quite good because it does not have the grain of ground glass, but it has to be thin if the focus of the projected image is not to suffer badly. Another useful material which is easily available is plastic tracing material used by draftsmen such as Kodatrace, several layers of this thin material can be sandwiched together and stuck down over a piece of clear glass — with the glass facing the projector. The white type needs no colour correction whereas the bluish tinted one requires a R30 colour correction filter. The colour temperature of the projector bulb should be 3200K for the correct colour reproduction of the transparency.

Your normal 35 mm slide projector is very suitable for this type of work and you can produce transparencies to fit in as backgrounds to a title or to a set. Those who are extremely ambitious can even project moving pictures frame by frame although it is advisable to use a 16 mm projector for this purpose. The camera movement is severely restricted when a back projected image is used on equipment designed for flat artwork shooting; and only zooming is possible. On the other hand when a back projected image is used as part of a solid set, then there is no restriction of the movement at all; the camera can pan, tilt, track, zoom, etc. It is also advisable to prepare your backgrounds on double-perforated stock so that the image can be reversed (flopped) if necessary.

Hotspot

Hotspot is the main problem with backprojection. If the projector is directed straight at the backprojection screen a hotspot will appear in the centre of the projected image. You can sometimes mask this off deliberately by carefully devising the set so that there is always something in the foreground to obscure this point. However it is much better to eliminate the hotspot altogether. Projecting via a front silvered mirror helps. In the case of a vertical set up, the screen is placed at the table top level and the mirror at 45° on the floor level below it. The projector can be positioned from the front or from the sides of the table. The image reversal is taken care of by flopping the transparency as required. The use of longer focal length projection lenses also helps to reduce the hotspot.

Lighting

The biggest drawback of this type of projection is created by lighting restrictions. Any light that reaches the projection screen washes out the image, so ideally there should be no other light present. This, of course, is possible in the case of a solid set up. Place the screen as far back as possible to avoid any light from the set spilling onto it. Use crosslighting to limit the light falling on the screen directly. This in itself creates further problems – the more the screen is moved back, the bigger it has to be and in addition to that the greater becomes the depth of field problem (i.e. keeping both the projected image and the foreground set in sharp focus).

Matting in animated characters

In the case of backprojection on a flat artwork set up, you can use no other lighting than from the projector. Despite this, it is possible to matte in animated figures into realistic or photographed backgrounds this way. Prepare the artwork on acetate cells and

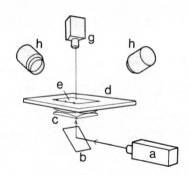

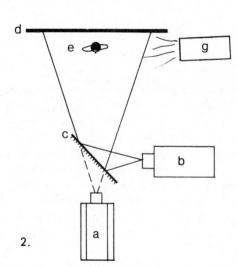

1, Back projection for a table set up. (a) Projector. (b) Front-surfaced mirror. (c) Condensers. (d) Animation table. (e) Focus plane. (g) Camera. (h) Normal top lighting.

2, Front projection system. (a) Camera on a nodal adaptor. (b) Projector. (c) Two-way mirror. (d) Highly reflective screen. (e) Subject. (g) Lights (directed onto the subject and away from the screen).

black out the animated figures on the reverse sides to ensure a complete opaqueness in the image area.

You shoot the background on a separate pass through the camera. Change the cels, and make all the movements *exactly* as planned for the pass when you photograph them. The cells placed over the backprojected image in the correct sequence produce a black silhouette of the figures. After shooting the background, wind back to the start of the shot, and put a sheet of black glossy paper over the backprojection screen. Now light the cels from above with polarised lighting as normal and photograph them against the black background and in perfect sync with the first pass to give a composite image.

Zoptic screen

This is a very recent development in backprojection which eliminates all the problems of lighting normally associated with this system. It can be used both for flat artwork animation and as background to a solid set. An animated sequence such as the one described above can be done in one single operation because the artwork can be lit from above without affecting the backprojected image in any way. You must still opaque the animated figures to prevent the backprojected image from ghosting.

Because it is a complete process in one, the balance between the top lights and the projected image can be matched so that the animated characters blend in. The exposure is determined by the top lights, and a grey scale placed on the table can be an additional aid. If the balance between the projected image and the top-lit cell or grey scale is correct then the exposure for the top-light will be the same as that for the backlight. The top-light exposure can of course be easily calculated so that a composite shot of this type could be photographed without any special testing prior to the actual shot. Cut out figures, titles and anything else can be placed on this screen and matted into the projected background in one single operation without windback. The only lighting consideration is that the toplight should be polarised.

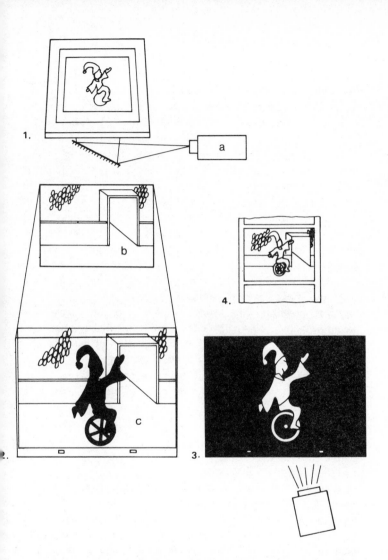

1, A slide can be projected from under the table via a 45° front silvered mirror. 2, Two passes through the camera are necessary to get a composite picture of a backprojected image and cel artwork. (a) Slide projector, (b) projected image, (c) cel artwork seen as silhouette. 3, Cel artwork top lit. 4, Composite image.

Zoptic screen in a model set

You can build the foreground sets near – or even in contact with the zoptic screen. Indeed a zoptic screen can be incorporated into foreground areas deliberately and the image projected from the side via a front silvered mirror. If it is fitted into the window area of the model house, you can project a live image into that area – even an 8 mm projector can be used in this case. Because the projection area is small compared to the total screen area the quality is equal to that obtained with the use of a 16 mm projector. When preparing the live inserts of this kind, shoot the required framing of the figure over the whole frame so that it does not need to be blown up when projected into a specific area, because this will result in poorer quality. Larger background areas should be prepared on 35 mm slides or 16 mm movie film because a certain amount of blowing up of the image will be required during the framing of close-ups of the foreground action.

You use polarising filters on all lights, and the exposure is governed by the incident light once a good visual balance has been achieved between the backprojected image and the rest of the set. You achieve the balance with N.D. filters to cut down the intensity of the lights on the projector. There are no restrictions to the camera movements so that zooming, panning, etc. can all be done over a composite image.

Aerial image projection

This technique involves the use of a pair of condensers which are placed in the backlight cutout of the animation table top. They are normally very expensive but an enthusiast may be able to find large condensers in surplus stores. In any case, it is well worth being acquainted with this technique in theory at least. The projected image is focused on the top surface of the condenser. The focusing operation needs a piece of grease-proof paper or similar material which placed in contact with this surface, because the image is not normally visible.

At one distance only, this image can be focused onto the film by the camera lens without any distortions. Animation cells placed on the condensers can be lit from above and photographed simultaneously with the projected image. This image is not affected by the light because it is focused by the condensers directly into the camera. It can be seen through the optics of the camera only. If a diffusion material is placed on the surface of the condenser the image becomes real as such is affected by any light from above. The camera movement is restricted totally and the size of the projected image is restricted in itself by the size of the condensers. Precision of the highest degree is required in the linking up of all the optical elements involved. Any misalignment creates vignetting problems.

Front projection

This system is based on the use of a highly reflective screen material which is similar to the material used in the manufacturing of car number-plates. The background image is projected from the front via a two-way mirror so that the camera lens can view the scene along the same axis along which the image is projected. The projected image is very weak compared with the set lighting. So it is "seen" by the camera *only* when reflected from the special material. The reflective properties of the screen are so much greater than any normal subjects that only the light reflected from the screen is visible and the light falling on the subject is not. Any object placed in front of the screen will be automatically matted into the projected picture. The subject needs to be lit so that a good balance between the projected image and foreground can be achieved. The exposure is determined by the incident light and is assumed to be correct for the projected image also if the two are properly balanced. Because the screen reflects the light straight back towards the projector, a certain amount of scatter light does not affect it and the image is not easily washed out. However the light cannot be allowed to fall directly onto the screen and this means that the foreground has to be lit by cross-lighting in order to avoid washing out the background image.

Your own optical printer?

One of the biggest drawbacks to getting sophisticated opticals for non-professional films is the cost. Laboratories and optical houses make considerable charges for this type of work on 16 mm, and hardly anything is done by them on 8 mm apart from straightforward reductions. However a projector of your own fitted with a stop-frame facility can enable you to do a number of fairly sophisticated opticals. The projector should preferably be 16 mm even when you are working on 8 mm. Old 16 mm projectors can be picked up at reasonable price and converted to this purpose.

Projector requirements

The projector must be able to register each frame accurately. Professional projectors used for this purpose have special movements which are the same as the high precision camera movements. Obviously you cannot expect to find that kind of precision in an ordinary 16 mm projector. However each make of projector has some form of registration even if it is the pull-down claw which remains engaged in the perforation at one specific point just after the frame has been pulled into position. This is normally sufficiently accurate for the type of work one is likely to attempt with such equipment. In addition to this the projector should be able to be driven from frame to frame at very slow speeds to ensure that it always stops at the same point. A stop-motion drive system similar to the one described earlier for use with some cameras is ideal for this purpose. Alternatively it can be operated manually; this is not really any more tedious than cel animation work where cels are changed for each frame.

If the projector has a mesh or grid filter to preserve the stationary film, obviously you have to remove that. A less powerful lamp and

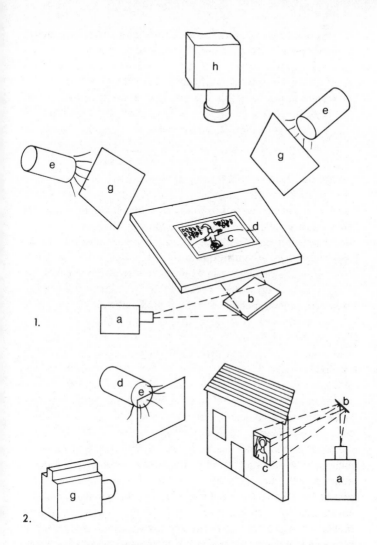

Composite images in one go! 1, Zoptic screen in use with cels. (a) Projector. (b) Mirror. (c) Zoptic screen. (d) Cel artwork. (e) Top lights. (g) Polarizing filters. (h) Camera.

2, Zoptic screen in use with miniatures. (a) Projector. (b) Mirror. (c) Zoptic screen. (d) Front light. (e) Polarizing filter. (g) Camera.

an extra heat absorbing glass will be a useful protection against overheating the film. When the film overheats in the projector gate it buckles and the focus is lost so it is advisable to take the frame (shoot) with your camera as soon as the projector has been moved on to the next frame. If you are going to take a rest it should be after the frame in the projector has been photographed because if it does buckle after that it won't matter.

The set up

A normal back-projection screen can be used, although the Zoptic screen offers the added advantage that titles can be placed over it and lit from the front and so incorporated into the projected image. A horizontal set up is perhaps the easiest to operate, but the projector can be placed underneath the animation table normally used for flat artwork animation as described earlier. For correct line up a grid should be placed in the projector gate to which the camera is then lined up.

Possible results

The results which can be achieved in this way will certainly give an added dimension to your films.

A 16 mm print can be copied directly onto 8 mm and titles, mixes and fades added. A freeze-frame can be introduced at a chosen point by simply photographing the same frame for as long as required.

Skip-framing can also be done to speed up or slow down the action.

Split-screening is also possible by copying a particular scene in one section of the frame only while the rest of the frame is masked off; on a second pass another scene can be copied in the un-exposed area of the frame or a title can be added. (Because the projected picture is in effect being reduced even an 8 mm projected image will reproduce well.)

Scenes can also be linked by means of wipes of various types using cut-out mattes to wipe out the outgoing scene and the complementary counter-mattes to reveal the incoming scene.

Even overlap printing can be done this way where the figure freezes at one end of the frame and the same figure emerges out of the frozen image and continues to move to the other side of frame. There are two crucial requirements for this type of printing: the background should be a perfect black and the figure should be cross-lit, or back-lit particularly when several images are to appear as a strobing trail behind the figure. One and the same positive image is used for this effect. Over a certain section, the image is repeated two or more frames later than on the first pass through the camera. (The extent of this stagger depends on the speed of the movement within the scene and the effect desired.) Alternatively the image can be frozen at one point by continually printing that same frame. On a second pass the camera is wound back to the point where the freeze starts and the rest of the scene is printed on from there.

Tinting the image

A certain amount of filtration will be necessary to ensure the correct reproduction of the projected image. However this can be overdone deliberately and complete scenes or some sections only (as well as sections of a frame only) can be tinted a particular colour by using progressively stronger filters.

One of the effects possible in this way is to achieve a total colour distortion of the image. For this purpose you should prepare a black-and-white positive and a black-and-white negative of your master scene. If the master is shot on 16 mm colour negative film then it is best to order from the laboratory a high-contrast print both from the original negative and from the colour positive which would normally have been made. This way you have obtained your images on black-and-white stock with very little difficulty and marginal expense. High-contrast positive and negative prints are best for this purpose, but ordinary monochromatic black-and-white stock as used for rush-printing by the laboratories is also satisfactory. It is most important that the scene chosen for this purpose should contain roughly equal amounts of dark and light tones and should be generally of a contrasty character.

The two black-and-white records of the master scene should be clearly identified and synchronised. The positive record is then laced up in the projector and printed through a strong filter. The film in the camera is then wound back to the start and the negative record is then printed through another strong filter. The results obtained this way give the reproduction of the original scene which is highly distorted in colour: all black areas are one strong colour and all white areas are made up of another strong colour – and all the inbetween areas appear as a third colour which is formed by the combination of the two strong colours used. The extent to which this effect of a third colour is pronounced will depend on the balance between the two colours used and it is absolutely essential to do a wedge test to determine this relationship precisely. This is done by wedging the positive record at ten (or more) frames interval and then the negative record is wedged per frame over each of the ten-frame segments. It is best to prepare a chart with the details of the wedges so that when you find just the frame you like you can easily trace the precise exposure for the two elements which is required to produce that particular result. Any imperfection in the registration of the positive and the negative records of the scene only contribute to the third-colour effect and you should not worry unduly about the possible lack of precision in your equipment. The high-contrast stock tends to pull towards a clear distinction between black and white at the expense of the grey areas which tend to break up. This also enhances the third colour because it is this pull between the two areas which creates the mismatch between the two images which results in the overlap areas which receive the light on both passes through the camera; and so they appear as outlines in the third colour; i.e. yellow if green and red are the two strong colours.

When this scene is finally inserted in your film it is best to introduce it as a long mix from the master scene with normal colour. That way the scene appears to distort gradually. Obviously the distorted scene and the original must be matched frame to frame so that the action within frame continues uninterrupted. Any slight mismatch in the size of the image is covered up by the distortion effect.

If you don't have a projector to attempt this sort of effect you might like to do the same thing with a still photograph on the enlarger. A matched mix from a normal colour photograph to another one with colour distortion can be also quite effective.

The Zoptic special effects device

This patented device is used mainly in conjunction with front-projection and is within the scope of major studios only. However the Zoptic effect is within the reach of the amateur when used as back projection in conjunction with the Zoptic screen which was developed for this purpose (see page 208).

The principle

The Zoptic principle consists of varying the size of the projected image while at the same time altering the area covered by the camera lens so that the projected image always fills the frame and therefore appears to be constant. Artwork, or models in front of the screen will then appear to grow in size, shrink, or even fly within the picture. A figure will appear to come towards the camera while in fact its relative distance from the camera remains unaltered.

The practice

In order to vary the size of the projected image the projector should ideally be fitted with a zoom lens. The total distance of the zoom is marked up on the zoom ring and divided by the number of frames. The camera, set at the same relative position to the projector on the other side of the screen, should also be equipped with a zoom lens. The centres of the projector lens and the camera lens should be set in a straight line and the screen is set as perfectly perpendicular to this line as possible in between them. The start and end positions of the zoom should be established by projecting the image at the two extreme sizes and lining up the camera so that at both points the projected image exactly fills the frame. These positions should then be marked on the zoom ring of the camera lens, and the distance between them divided by the number of frames to give the appropriate increments. A check should be made at several points to ensure that the two zooms are reasonably matched.

Tracking instead of zooming

You may be lucky in being able to use a projector already fitted with a zoom lens or have one which will take a zoom lens without difficulty. For those less lucky the alternative is to mount the projector on a horizontal tracking device (as discussed earlier in conjunction with cameras). This track should be set perpendicular to the screen and the projector is moved towards the screen. Focusing should be done manually for each frame using a carefully calibrated scale. The camera can still use the zoom lens only each change of position of the projector (and therefore each change in the size of the projected picture) should be checked and calibrated on the camera zoom ring. Alternatively the camera too can be tracked along in the same way as the projector.

Practical problems

When the projector is closer to the screen the image appears brighter than when it is at the farther position. This also applies when the zoom lens is used. It is therefore important for the projector lens to be fitted with an iris. The brightness of the projector light should be measured at the widest picture area and it should be cut down by using the iris until the reading is the same at the smallest size of the projected image. The iris ring is then calibrated to give a gradual change from one position to the other during the shot so that there is no appreciable difference in the exposure of the projected image during the shot. The model or puppet in front of the screen or the flat artwork in contact with it is lit to match the projected image in brightness and in such a way that it appears to form part of the projected picture. The key to this lies in establishing first the source and direction of light in the background picture and then matching this as closely as possible with your lighting.

Model aeroplanes can really fly this way . . . puppets can grow to giant sizes . . . Coloured lettering forming a title can fly in towards the camera etc . . .

Slit-scan

The cameras fitted with a time exposure facility and a motorised zoom lens already have all the basic ingredients for slit-scan shooting.

The slit-scan exploits the drift away from the centre during a zoom-in which we have come across earlier. A dot of light placed a little distance away from the lens centre (frame centre) will move towards the edge of frame when the lens is zoomed in. If the camera shutter is left open during this time as for exposure, then this dot will have registered as a line on the film. By the same principle a line will produce a two-dimensional shape and a rectangular shape will produce a three-dimensional effect.

A static slit

The slits can be made up of various shapes, and these shapes could even be altered during the shooting. A static slit in the form of a straight line is perhaps the easiest but it will never be able to fully cover the frame. This is not necessarily a disadvantage

219

because the blank area of frame can be used to insert another image, a title, or even a different type of slit-scan pattern. A circular-shaped slit positioned at the centre of frame and big enough to reach the edges of frame when the lens is fully zoomed in will cover the greater part of the frame area. Even so the inner area will still remain black. This too can be used to insert another image. Static slits can also be traced around the particular shapes within the frame, e.g. outline of a face, or some architectural object. When carefully positioned the slit-scan effect will appear to emanate from these objects when it is overlaid over them.

Moiré patterns and mosaics made up of pieces of coloured gelatine should be placed behind the slit. This way the outline is transformed into a series of points of light of various colours instead of a continuous unbroken slit. On zooming, with the shutter open, each one of these points of light will trace a line towards the edge of frame. In-between each frame the coloured pattern should be moved a little to give a continuously changing effect. The slit-scan effect produced this way consists of a series of straight lines. However, if the coloured patterns behind the static slit could also be moved during the exposure (i.e. the zoom) then a much more sophisticated effect can be obtained. Multicoloured shapes are created which then move in an outward direction when the artwork (coloured pattern) is moved on a little in between each frame (this is apart from the set movement during the zoom). Whilst synchronising the start of the zoom with the shutter opening can be performed reasonably accurately manually, the syncronisation of the movement of the patterns is much more difficult.

A simple solenoid device can be used to activate the shutter mechanism and the zoom can be activated simultaneously. The shutter is closed at the end of the zoom and the next time it is activated a new frame will be in the camera gate. This operation can be performed both zooming in and out although the artwork must be moved on in the same direction in between each frame. An ordinary motorised zoom cannot easily be synchronised with another motor which would drive the artwork continuously backwards and forwards always starting and finishing at the same time as the shutter is opened and closed. Those familiar with electronic servo systems may be adventurous enough to consider fitting this type of drive to run both the zoom lens and the carriage carrying the artwork. Once this becomes possible, then the slit itself can be mounted on this carriage so that it can scan the full length of the frame while the artwork remains static during the shooting and is only moved on a little in between frames. With a moving slit many other possibilities emerge. You can use the projected image in place of your artwork and instead of moving the artwork on in between frames the projector is advanced by a frame and the change in the pre-filmed images produces the necessary change within the slit-scan pattern. And what's to stop you from projecting a live-action picture.

Index